THE REFERENCE SHELF   VOLUME 43 NUMBER 5

JAPAN

ASIAN POWER

EDITED BY

IRWIN ISENBERG

Assistant Resident Representative
The United Nations Development Program in India

THE H. W. WILSON COMPANY

NEW YORK 1971

THE REFERENCE SHELF

The books in this series contain reprints of articles, excerpts
from books, and addresses on current issues and social trends in the
United States and other countries. There are six separately bound
numbers in each volume, all of which are generally published in
the same calendar year. One number is a collection of recent
speeches; each of the others is devoted to a single subject and gives
background information and discussion from various points of
view, concluding with a comprehensive bibliography. Books in the
series may be purchased individually or on subscription.

Library of Congress Cataloging in Publication Data

Isenberg, Irwin, comp.
  Japan: Asian power.

  (The Reference shelf, v. 43, no. 5)
  Bibliography: p.
  1. Japan--History--1868-   2. Japan--Economic
conditions--1945-   3. Japan--Foreign relations--
1945-   I. Title. II. Series.
DS881.9.I75   915.2   70-159162
ISBN 0-8242-0450-6

PREFACE

It was only a quarter century ago that the island nation of Japan lay in ruins, its dreams of an empire in Asia shattered, its economy smashed, its cities in ashes, its population stunned by the total defeat of World War II.

But reconstruction was swift and recovery so rapid that by the middle 1950s, only a decade after the war's end, Japan was poised for the economic takeoff that transformed it into the world's third most productive economic power, after the United States and the Soviet Union. In fact, Japan's long-term growth rate of 10 to 14 percent a year has been so phenomenal that some economists predict the country will come close to rivaling US living standards by the end of this century.

Many factors have contributed to this success story. Japan is a remarkably homogeneous nation; its people are well educated and appear to have an almost unlimited capacity for work and self-discipline; its industrialists and financiers combine caution and imagination in a way that stimulates the economy and produces spectacular results; its government is stable and led by responsible political leaders; its defense expenditures are minimal, as the country relies on the umbrella of US military power. As a result of this combination of favorable circumstances, the Land of the Rising Sun has plunged into an age of unprecedented prosperity and progress.

At the same time, Japan is a land of delicate beauty and highly stylized cultural forms that lend its landscape and people a charm and serenity that sometimes seem at odds with the country's headlong rush into the world of mass consumer production, traffic jams, pollution, and computerized technology. For the moment at least, a majority of Japanese do not seem to be having any great difficulty in

3

fitting the technology of the industrialized society into the traditional patterns of their culture.

However, as a result of their emergence as an economic superpower, the Japanese are faced with many important questions, the answers to which will shape the destiny of the country in the decades to come. How long is Japan to rely on the US military umbrella? What will or should be Japan's political and economic role in Asia? What will be the course of its relations with mainland China and the Soviet Union?

This book discusses these and other issues. The first section sketches some of the major historical trends that have shaped the Japanese society and economy. From this section it can be seen that the ingredients for Japan's success were present long ago and did not appear on the scene suddenly during the US occupation after World War II, as is sometimes erroneously supposed. Japan's industrialization process was set in motion a century ago. Similarly, reforms in government administration and in education were begun in the nineteenth century and these changes, too, became part of the foundation on which modern Japan rests.

The second section offers a broad view of Japan in terms of its political, economic, and sociological context. This section also looks to the future for indications of the direction in which Japanese society may move.

The third section presents a detailed analysis of the Japanese economy—how it runs, what makes it tick, and what it has achieved. These articles show that Japan's economy is powerfully diversified and has spread its roots far and deep throughout Asia and much of the rest of the world.

The last section views Japan's relations with the world in terms of military and geopolitical implications which, however, cannot be divorced from economics. Clearly, Japan's relations with the United States are central. But Japan's changing role in Asia may result in altered ties between Tokyo and Washington as well as in a new position of leadership for Japan in Asia.

President Nixon's trip to China and the changes which will occur in US-Chinese relations are also bound to have a major effect on Japan. Moreover, Japan's disappointment about not being informed in advance about the new US economic policy, which aims to correct balance-of-payment deficits and which has serious implications for Japan, will also produce a new diplomatic climate.

The editor wishes to thank the authors and publishers who have given their permission to reprint the articles included in this volume.

IRWIN ISENBERG

October 1971

CONTENTS

IV. JAPAN AND THE WORLD

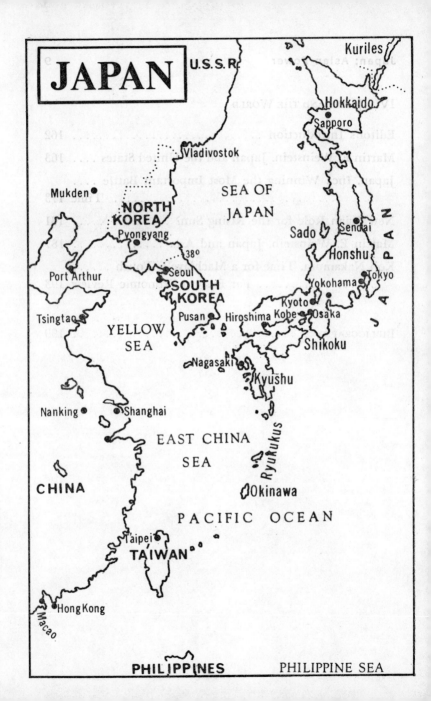

I. JAPAN IN PERSPECTIVE

EDITOR'S INTRODUCTION

The destruction-to-riches story of postwar Japan cannot be fully understood without some knowledge of the country's history and its value system, both of which contain the seeds from which Japan has flowered into an economic Goliath. Whereas many Japanese once believed that the prosperity of their nation depended upon the possession of colonies and spheres of influence in Asia, it now appears clear that the country's prosperity, in reality, stems in part from character traits and a social system which are conducive to progress and growth. Of course, the reforms stimulated by the US occupation forces after World War II also played an enormous role in the shaping of contemporary Japan.

This section attempts to put modern Japan into some perspective by sketching in the country's history and culture. The first article, which appeared in the *Unesco Courier*, outlines the momentous changes set in motion by the Meiji Emperor, who opened Japan to Western ideas and technology and constructed a sound economic and administrative base for national development. The next selection, detailing the growth of Japanese technology in the past century, also speaks of the efforts made to improve the quality of education and to stimulate the development of human resources in all scientific fields.

There follows a review of the history and development of Edo, which is present-day Tokyo. Edo has grown from a small fishing village to the world's largest city; however, as the author stresses, Tokyo is faced with the same problems that plague large urban conglomerates everywhere. The last article is a brief compendium of facts about different aspects of Japanese life and culture. It outlines the major religions

in Japan and various important cultural features, such as
the Kabuki theatre, the puppet theatre, and the tea ceremony. The reader is reminded that for all its advanced technology and modernity, Japan still places the highest value
on its ancient and traditional cultural forms.

EMPEROR MEIJI—FATHER OF MODERN JAPAN [1]

Early in 1868 a young man whom the world was to know
as the Emperor Meiji [i.e., enlightened peace] emerged into
history from behind the curtain of courtiers and ceremony
that had for centuries isolated the Japanese throne.

For more than two hundred years Japan had remained
a closed country, ruled by Shoguns (military governors)
who had reduced the emperor to a figurehead. But by the
middle of the nineteenth century this self-enforced isolation
of Japan suddenly came to an end. Besieged by foreign
powers clamoring for the country to open up to Western
commerce, and threatened by rebellious feudal lords, the
fifteenth Tokugawa Shogun yielded power to the Imperial
house.

The youthful Meiji Emperor, Mitsuhito, and his dynamic advisers opened Japan not only to Western ideas and
commerce but to all the tempestuous currents of the nineteenth century world. The Meiji Restoration . . . was like
the bursting of a dam behind which had accumulated the
energies and forces of centuries. Japan set out to achieve
in only a few decades what had taken centuries to develop
in the West: the creation of a modern nation, with modern
industries and political institutions, and a modern pattern
of society.

Young Samurai changed their Japanese dress for top hats
and dark suits and sailed off to Europe and America to
study Western techniques of government, industry—and war.
In a tour de force of modernization, the Meiji revolutionaries

[1] From article by Ki Kumura, a Japanese historian and novelist. *Unesco
Courier.* 21:4+. S. '68.

raised their country to be a peer of the Western powers, in less than forty years—and without sacrificing Japan's traditional culture.

The events leading to the Restoration started the year after Meiji was born, when Commodore Matthew Perry's "black ships" from the United States steamed into Kurihama Bay in 1853 on a mission of diplomacy and commerce.

After Perry signed a treaty of amity with the Shogun the next spring, Russia, the Netherlands and Great Britain secured similar agreements. Hermit Japan, after secluding itself for over two hundred years, slowly began to resume contact with the outside world.

When Japan reopened its doors, it was stagnating under a feudal system which had divided society into four distinct castes: warriors, farmers, artisans and tradesmen. So all-pervasive was this caste system that it exercised control over the very lives of the people to the extent of prescribing exact rules on all activities relating to daily life and behavior. Even the use of language, both written and spoken was de·termined by the individual's social class.

The Confucian ethic, with its emphasis on the practice and cultivation of the cardinal virtues of filial piety, kindness, righteousness, propriety, intelligence, and faithfulness, constituted the foundation on which all relations between superiors and inferiors, one's obedience to authority, and the concept of master-servant were formalized. Society was stable, but totally immobilized.

The Japan of those days was moreover an impoverished agrarian state. Even in the late 1870s, some 75 to 80 percent of the employed population were engaged in agriculture. Per capita annual income was estimated at about $65. In other words, Japan was a nation sustained by a farming community working at a bare subsistence level.

Right from the time of Perry and the first treaties the Japanese were interested in international relations on the basis of independence and equality. There was a danger, they felt, that the Great Powers might dominate them, and a way of thinking, not in terms of the clan but in terms of the state, was born from this feeling.

The confrontation between groups advocating an open-door policy and those who urged the exclusion of foreigners was, for a time, bitter. Both factions had the same goal: to preserve national independence. When the champions of seclusion realized that this freedom could be maintained only through intercourse with foreigners, they made common cause with their former opponents.

Conflict also arose over whether Japan should return political power to the throne or continue the traditional Shogunate system of government. Again, national independence was the determining factor.

In 1867, both the Shogun and Emperor Komei, Meiji's father, died. The young Emperor and the new Shogun, Yoshinobu were duly installed in the highest offices of the land.

Yoshinobu was a man of vision, convinced that Japanese independence hinged on the country being unified and modernized. In late 1867, encouraged by a coalition of fiefs led by the strong provincial clans known as the "Satcho Dohi," he surrendered his authority to the Emperor and ended seven hundred years of military rule.

In February 1868, the Reformation began: Emperor Meiji assumed supreme executive authority, and informed foreign representatives that his title should replace the Shogun's in all existing treaties.

Encouraged by his counselors, many of whom he chose from the Samurai, Japan's warrior class, Meiji broke the strict prohibition which barred foreigners from the capital, Kyoto, and received the representatives of the Great Powers in a New Year's audience. He also cast away the feudal edict against travel, and journeyed the twenty-seven miles from Kyoto to Osaka to attend a naval review.

His major step in the first year of the Reformation came when he summoned his nobles to the royal palace and, in their presence, took the "charter oath" by which he prom-

ised that a deliberative assembly would be formed, all classes
would share in the government, and that justice, not ancient
custom, would in future be the guiding principle of the administration.

In the same year, he separated Japan further from its
past by moving the capital from Kyoto to Edo and renaming
it Tokyo, or Eastern Capital. [See "Tokyo—A Tale of Two
Cities," in this section, below.—Ed.]

In the beginning, the Reformation's leaders devoted almost all their energies to developing a sound economic base
for the new state: the monetary system had to be stabilized,
taxes levied, new industry developed, and foreign markets
opened.

One prerequisite change was the abolition of the feudal
system which, with autocratic chieftains governing and levy-
ing taxes over huge estates, stood squarely in the way of
economic progress. No central government could effectively
unify Japan if it continued to exist.

Feudalism had been a way of life since the twelfth century, and the clans were strong. Yet such was the spirit of
the times that the four great Satcho Dohi clans of the west
returned their estates to the Emperor in 1869, and entreated
him to reorganize them under a uniform set of laws. The
lesser clans soon followed, and between 1871 and 1872 the
four classes of warrior, artisan, farmer and tradesman were
abolished.

The most important factor in Japan's economic development was a strong and integrated control by the central
government. This strength was needed to enforce three difficult decisions made in the first half of Meiji's reign, and
which were to have enduring effects on Japan's prosperity.

First, the government resisted the temptation to unite
the country through foreign military adventures. Six years
after the young Emperor took power, strong members of the
government favored going to war with Korea after Korean
shore batteries had fired on a Japanese gunboat. Despite the
fact that such action would have temporarily unified the

country, which was plagued by discontented elements at the time, the proposal was rejected in 1873, and the nation's energies were turned to solving domestic problems.

The second decision was to deflate the economy in 1881. Serious inflation at that time made it difficult to promote modern industry and investment. Disregarding public dissatisfaction, the Meiji government firmly introduced stringent fiscal measures that halted inflation in 1884, with the result that the economic goals set in 1868 were achieved in 1885, as planned.

The third decision concerned the financing of new industry. The Meiji leaders avoided the comparatively easy solution of allowing foreign investment, reasoning that it might make Japan dependent on foreign nations. Instead, they raised the necessary funds by instituting a land tax. Investment from abroad was restricted.

Meiji Japan built its modern industry on a traditional foundation. Raw silk and tea were the original mainstays of Japan's exports, and these were encouraged (even the Empress set up a cocoonery in the palace grounds to promote sericulture) because their foreign exchange earning power helped establish new industries.

Hokkaido, then a vast virgin island at the north of the Japanese archipelago, was opened up with American assistance. Agriculture and Japan's chemical industry (today the second in the world) were started. Apple trees, never before seen in Japan, were planted, and the first dairy industry was begun.

After seeing its success in the West, the Meiji leaders believed firmly in private enterprise. But centuries of feudalism had left the country with few industrial traditions or skills, and Japanese investors were cautious about risking their capital in new and sometimes strange ventures.

To foster industrial growth, joint-stock companies were encouraged, with emphasis on foreign-exchange firms, trading companies and transportation companies; government subsidies were granted to key businesses and industries, and favorable tax concessions made.

The government also built model factories in the steel, cement, plate glass, firebrick, woolen textiles and spinning industries. They were set up on a profit-making basis but with the primary aim of introducing European production methods and techniques into Japan.

In all its efforts to modernize industry, the Reformation leaders were aided and encouraged by Emperor Meiji who traveled throughout the islands, inspecting shipyards, opening factories, and visiting development areas.

Reforms in other fields were far reaching: education was made compulsory, all restrictions were lifted on Japanese going abroad, Christianity was permitted, vaccinations, postal service, telegraphs, and steamships were introduced, torture was abolished, European dress was prescribed for officials (with the Emperor showing the way by adopting Western military dress), and European and American advisers were freely employed.

Great efforts were made in the field of education; the government knew that for Japan to be wealthy and strong, the intellectual level of the people had to be raised. The Japanese appetite for knowledge had already been whetted under the Tokugawa Shoguns when private temple schools flourished, and the study of Western science, primarily in the medical field, was pursued through Nagasaki, the only city open to foreign trade.

Before the Reformation, education had progressed to the point where 50 percent of the male population and 15 percent of the female population had received some formal instruction.

A policy of equal opportunity was established in Meiji Japan. To draw gifted students from poor homes, education was made free at military academies and teacher-training schools and colleges. ...

In 1890, the Emperor ordered that the guiding principles of school education be compiled in an "Imperial Rescript on Education." It enjoined all students to honor their ancestors, respect their parents, be loyal to superiors and serve their country.

That the educational policy was successful can be seen from the fact that by 1885, 42 percent of the students at Tokyo Imperial University were commoners compared to 25 percent in 1878, and at the end of the Meiji era, primary school attendance was 95 percent.

This love of learning of the Japanese people, coupled with an academic level which was extremely advanced, although limited to a narrow sphere, provided the conditions necessary, once Western instruction was introduced, to bring about an amazing dissemination of general education, and produced scholars of international caliber.

Dr. Hideyo Noguchi, who was destined to become a world-famous bacteriologist in tropical diseases, started from humble beginnings as the son of a very poor farmer. Other distinguished scientists of the Meiji era were Jokichi Takamine who synthesized adrenalin, Shibasaburo Kitazato who isolated the gangrene bacteria, and Kiyoshi Shiga who isolated the dysentery germ.

Japan's modernization was carried out to counter the impact of the West, and the much needed reforms were mainly instituted by the strong central government. Yet, those outside the government, including its critics, also worked effectively for Japan's renewal.

For example, Yukichi Fukuzawa, a pioneer educator, in expressing his opposition to the tendency toward an increasing governmental predominance, established Japan's first private institution of higher learning, Keio University. Nevertheless, he was always concerned with the independence of the state and, as an educator, he worked for its betterment by increasing the capabilities of his fellow Japanese.

Emori Ueki, a prominent liberal politician, was another example of "creative opposition." While severely criticizing the authoritarian Meiji government by preaching freedom and equality, he declared that any person who did not extend his capacities and utilize his talents was failing the nation.

Taisuke Itagaki, another liberal of the Reformation, was tireless in his efforts to persuade the government to institute a deliberative assembly, and in 1881 it issued an edict declaring that a national parliament would be established in 1890 with the intervening nine years to be devoted to government preparations for an orderly change.

Hirobumi Ito, one of the statesmen who played a major role in reshaping Japan, was sent to Europe in the same year to study Western governments, and determine which one should serve as the model for Japan. After evaluating the American, British, and French systems, he chose the Imperial German constitution as best suited for Japan's needs. It provided for an elected assembly, but made the government responsible to the throne. In 1889, Emperor Meiji promulgated the new constitution, and one year later the legislature was convened.

Parallel to governmental, social and industrial progress, the Japanese took on the considerable task of persuading their foreign treaty partners to revise the terms of their agreements. The existing treaties, which favored the foreign signatories with low import duties (mostly 5 percent), and gave their citizens exemption from Japanese law courts, had been signed under vastly different conditions.

It took eleven years for Japan to get the terms it wanted. The break came when Great Britain finally agreed to a new treaty abolishing extraterritoriality, and giving Japan the right to set its own import tariffs. Similar treaties with other countries were soon concluded, and the Emperor fixed 1899 as the year that they would come into force.

During this time, foreign wars had been avoided, but in 1894-1895, Japan declared war on China over Korea and defeated the Chinese on the battlefield. In 1904 hostilities broke out with Russia, Japanese troops entering Manchuria. A peace treaty was signed the following year.

During the remainder of Emperor Meiji's reign, Japan moved within the circle of great powers consolidating its position as a vital component of international politics and trade.

On July 30, 1912, Emperor Meiji died at the age of fifty-nine. Under him, Japan had emerged from behind the ritual screen that had shielded it from the rest of the world to become the leading power in Asia and a peer of the West.

The revolution that Meiji presided over was even more remarkable in that it was orderly and controlled, and enhanced the monarchy rather than destroyed it, a result mainly due to the capable leaders who, in this period of "Enlightened Rule," shaped the new Japan.

FROM CHRYSANTHEMUM TO ELECTRONIC COMPUTER [2]

Japan is the world's leading shipbuilder, second greatest producer of motor vehicles and electronics, and third largest producer of steel. It is the leading exporter of textiles and textiles machines: 20 percent of the world's staple fibers are made there. And it is a major fishing nation with an annual catch of twelve million tons.

Yet only 15 percent of Japan is arable, and below the surface of the land, there are few mineral resources, the basis on which most industrialized countries are built.

The phenomenon of modern Japan is due to many reasons, not the least of which are the industry and intelligence of its people. But equally important is their unique ability to rise to the challenge of foreign culture, while maintaining their own identity.

When the Meiji Reformation initiated its open-door policy to the West, the tools of Occidental civilization the Japanese seized most eagerly were science and technology. Using them with skill and imagination, they built their country into Asia's foremost industrial nation, in just thirty years.

[2] From article in *Unesco Courier.* 21:24-7. S. '68.

Despite the curtain of isolation arbitrarily run down around the island empire by its feudal government, Western science found its way into Japan in 1823, when Philip Franz von Siebold, a German medical officer in the service of the Dutch (the only Westerners allowed to maintain contact during Japan's national seclusion) opened a school in Nagasaki to teach medicine and botany.

He was expelled from Japan in 1829 when he was found in possession of a map of the country, at that time a serious offense for foreigners. However, the seed of modern learning was planted, and one of his students, Takano Choei, became a distinguished scholar of Western sciences, spreading the new knowledge mainly through his translations into Japanese of European scientific works.

Near the end of the feudal government's rule, a research institute for "foreign" sciences was established in 1853 where astronomy, geology, physics, mathematics and chemistry, as well as Western languages, were taught. Science instruction was also started at two military schools. Industry, in the form of blast and reverberatory furnaces, and iron and cotton mills, was also begun.

When the imaginative Meiji leaders came to power in 1867, their approach to science and technology stemmed from their policy of strengthening the nation by "seeking knowledge far and wide." They brought modern science to Japan by importing not only books but brains: almost six hundred Western engineers, lured by salaries as high as $2,000 a month, as well as the challenge of modernizing a medieval country, came from the West to direct new technological projects.

Although six government ministries were involved in promoting science and technology, the leading body in the early years of the Reformation was the Ministry of Technology which established the railway and telegraph services, managed government plants and mines, built lighthouses, and promoted the education of Japanese engineers, mainly through its administration of the school of technology, founded in 1871 and later amalgamated with Tokyo Imperial University.

The Imperial University was Japan's first university in the true sense that research as well as education was carried out. Founded in 1877, it became the leading center for training modern scientists and engineers. Foreign instructors were predominant in the beginning, with twelve of the fifteen professors of science coming from abroad.

Various countries influenced various disciplines: mathematics, physics and chemistry developed chiefly under the influence of the United States and Great Britain, medicine under Germany, and agriculture, biology, geology and mineralogy almost equally under Britain, the United States and Germany.

As science was being brought to Japan by foreign experts, Japanese students were being sent abroad to study. The main aim of the government in sending the students abroad was to train them as teachers, and in 1884 they started to replace foreign instructors. By 1893, scientific education had passed completely into the hands of Japanese professors.

Since the modernization of industry was forcibly initiated by the Meiji government, its role was important in the development of science and technology, especially the latter. Through the national research institutes attached to each government ministry, research and development was encouraged, promoted and systemized, especially with a view to improving industrial technology.

Development at this time in the various branches of science included: ... land surveying by the Bureau of Geography, established in 1871; the founding of the Tokyo Meteorological Observatory in 1875, which had twenty meteorological stations in operation by 1900; the formation of the Japan Seismology Society in 1880, the first such organization in the world; and research work in physics and biology.

Edward Sylvester Morse was a major contributor to Japanese biology. He arrived from the United States in 1877 to find that "evolution," whose principles had been enunciated by Charles Darwin twenty years before, was an unknown concept. He introduced it in his lectures and public meetings, and the idea was spread further by Japanese scientists.

In the early 1890s, about the time Japanese professors were replacing Westerners in the academic structure, Japanese scientists began to come into their own.

Perhaps the first creative Japanese chemist was Jokichi Takamine who discovered and synthesized adrenalin in 1900, and the enzyme, Taka-Diastase, in 1909; in 1910, another chemist, Umetaro Suzuki, discovered vitamin B; Nantaro Nagoka took Japan's first step in the direction of nuclear physics when he published his "Theory on Atom Structure" in 1903; Shibasaburo Kitazato's Institute for Research of Infectious Diseases, founded in 1892, was regarded as one of the world's three leading research institutes. The Japanese, although still striving to reach the level of Western science, began to reap the fruits of their intellectual industry and determination.

At the end of the nineteenth century, with the development of the textile, shipbuilding and machine industries, the manufacture of iron, coal mining, and the electric power industry, Japan gradually caught up with Western industrial powers.

By 1919, manufacturing had surpassed agriculture as Japan's most important economic activity, and the industrial "center of gravity" shifted to heavy and chemical industries.

World War I had a profound effect on Japanese science. Until then, it had developed in step with the West, but with international relations disrupted, Japan's scientists for the first time charted an independent course. Research institutions were founded during and immediately after the war and through them science was finally harnessed to technique and industry to serve as a driving force for progress.

Post-World War I scientific achievements were numerous: in physics, research into metals, especially new steels, aided Japanese industry, and nuclear physics made rapid progress with Hideki Yukawa presenting his "Theory of Mesotrons" in 1934 (for which he received Japan's first Nobel Prize in 1949). The second Nobel Prize awarded to a Japanese went to another physicist, Shinichiro Tomanaga in 1965.

In geophysics, Japan continued to pioneer seismological research; in biology, Kenjiro Fujii did outstanding research on chromosomes; in medicine, advances in the study of cancer were remarkable, beginning with the artificial generation of cancer in 1915 and later studies of liver cancer; in chemistry and agriculture, diligent investigations often had direct bearing on industry and food production.

However, this new maturity was to bear too little positive results in the decades that followed: Japanese scientific and industrial efforts were subordinated in the early 1930s to the military establishment, which led the country to defeat in World War II.

For several years after the war, scientific and technological research activities in Japan were virtually suspended. American occupation forces banned research on atomic energy, armaments, and aeronautics, and dismantled Japan's cyclotron.

In 1951, the peace treaty was signed, and in 1954 research in atomic physics and the development of atomic energy were resumed. The Science and Technology Agency was established in 1956 to coordinate activities in those fields, and in the same year Japan's Atomic Energy Commission was formed.

About 1955, Japan's postwar prosperity began and, recognizing the indispensability of science and technology to the resurging economy, the government and private enterprise built new universities, faculties and research institutes.

There was a conspicuous reliance in Japan at that time on foreign techniques, but efforts were started, and are being continued, by industry to redress this situation through financing scientific and technological research at universities, and expanding or establishing their own research institutions.

Poor conditions for study impose great restrictions on the development of basic research. This has resulted in a great many Japanese scientists going abroad in search of better research facilities, a situation that has hardly improved, especially in mathematics, physics and chemistry.

Although there are many universities in Japan, most of them were raised to their present status during postwar reforms and they are inferior in equipment to those founded before the war. When the education reform started in 1949, Japan had 172 science and technological facilities: by 1963 they had increased to 263, 130 national, 29 public, and 104 private.

In 1963, there were 107 research institutes attached to the universities, used jointly by all three types of universities for basic research.

Apart from these centers, there are about 80 national research institutes, attached to government ministries, which do basic research as well as conduct other investigations in such fields as public health, disaster prevention, industrial technology, etc.

Between 1953 and 1965, Japan increased its expenditure on scientific and technological research nine times to . . . [$1.18 billion]. Private sources provided more money than the government, whose research spending on defense is low, compared to other countries, accounting for only about 1 percent. In fact, industry spent almost three times the government amount on research in 1963-64. However latest figures show that the Japanese government is increasing its share: in 1967-68, official spending on research and development rose by almost 15 percent.

The government, for the most part, finances the national and public universities since tuition fees and other incomes amount to only 5 percent of their expenses. Private universities, attended by 70 percent of Japan's students in higher education, depend mainly on tuition fees for their financing, and in order to secure the necessary funds, they enroll many students—some maintain, too many. Their facilities are not

as good as the national universities, so the government has
instituted special subsidies to assist them with equipment
expenses and student research.

Although science and technology students have increased
twice as fast (between 1954 and 1964) as students in other
faculties, their numbers need to be greatly increased, and
an enrollment of a further 170,000 is planned.

Possible reasons for the shortage of students may be the
comparatively modest salaries and the system of remunera-
tion of Japanese scientists and engineers, particularly early
on in their careers. Pay is largely based on status and se-
niority, and there is insufficient recognition of talent. . . .

Despite these problems, Japan has been able to develop
into one of the six most advanced technological countries of
the world. The key industry in this prodigious rise has been
electronics, where Japan's output is second only to the USA's.

In 1966, Japan produced over . . . [$3 billion] worth of
electronics, 30 percent of which was exported. In telecommunications, the country's microwave networks are second
largest in the world, and handle all television broadcasts and
half the telephone transmissions. Japan's 100 million people
have 13 million telephones and 20 million TV receivers.

The best-known product of Japan's electronics industry
is the transistor radio, a now commonplace instrument of
communication that has had far-reaching effects on listening
habits throughout the world. . . .

Computers . . . are the core of Japan's electronics industry, in the absence of any large defense or space program,
and Japan uses more computers than any other nation. Its
first automatic computer was built in 1952, and a current
ambitious program, to build an ultrahigh performance computer system, began with state aid in 1966.

Japan has also been a leading nation in the development
of peaceful uses of nuclear energy. In 1967, the Japanese
Atomic Energy Commission began a big new ten-year program of research, development and utilization, with an estimated budget of over . . . [$1.2 billion]. Nuclear power

installations are to be increased with a target capacity of 6,000 megawatts for 1975, and between 30,000 and 40,000 MW for 1985.

Also in 1967, the keel was laid for Japan's first nuclear ship, an 8,300-ton vessel . . .

To keep Japan's economy vigorous, a "Medium-Term Economic Plan" was introduced in 1965. Among the scientific measures which were recommended in support of it were: the need to couple the advancement of science and technology with Japan's economic growth, improve the quality of scientists and engineers, increase research in public welfare, raise the level of technological work in agriculture, forestry and fisheries, and the smaller enterprises, assist and encourage research by tax relief, and improve the research environment.

This last mentioned is no mere platitude. A complete new "Science City" north of Tokyo, is to be completed by the mid-1970s. Its residents will be 52,000 scientists and engineers working in forty laboratories, to improve the world around us.

TOKYO—A TALE OF TWO CITIES [3]

Tokyo epitomizes the achievements of the century which has passed since the Meiji Restoration. It also reveals a city which confronts some of the most severe problems facing any great metropolis.

Prior to 1868 the city was called Edo, possibly after a local warrior who built a fort there. A small settlement existed in the twelfth century, but 1457 is generally regarded as the year in which Edo's history begins because it was then that Ota Dokan completed the first castle on the site now occupied by the Imperial Palace.

The castle had a position which commanded the land and sea routes from the Kanto plain to the west. It was this

[3] From article by William A. Robson, an urban planning authority. *Unesco Courier.* 21:49-50+. S. '68.

strategic reason which led Ieyasu Tokugawa to make the castle his principal seat when he took it over in 1590. When Ieyasu became Shogun in 1603 Edo became the administrative center of his military government. The Emperor remained at Kyoto with his Court, but power had shifted to Edo.

Edo was a small fishing village until the end of the sixteenth century. Then it began to grow. The Shogun summoned some 80,000 Samurai warriors to live in the city as his praetorian guard. The feudal lords were required to reside in the city every alternate year, and when they went to their fiefs they had to leave their wives and children behind as hostages. This led to the building of great houses, temples and shrines in Edo, and craftsmen, tradesmen, retainers and laborers crowded into the city.

By 1613 the population had grown to 150,000. In 1721 it was 1.3 million and by the end of the eighteenth century it had reached 1.5 million. This made Edo larger than any other city in the world except Peking. Since then fluctuations in the number of inhabitants have been exceptionally great, partly owing to natural disasters, and partly owing to political, military and economic events.

In 1868 a vital change of status was brought about when Edo became the capital of Japan in place of Kyoto. The Emperor took up residence in the castle, which became the Imperial Palace, and the name of the city was changed to Tokyo (Eastern Capital).

Modernization began with extraordinary rapidity: the telegraph was introduced in 1869, the telephone in 1871, the steam train the following year, gas street lights in 1874. Tokyo University was founded in 1877. The electric lamp made its appearance in 1878, and motorcars in 1903. The first electric railway started in 1910.

Yet the immediate effect of the Meiji Restoration on the size of the city was a sharp fall in the population. This was due to the exodus of the dispossessed Samurai and the feudal lords (daimyo) and their families, who owned more than half of the city. In 1872 the population had fallen to a little over half a million and it did not reach a million again until about 1880.

The seeds of rapid growth were, however, germinating, for Tokyo soon became an industrial, commercial, financial and cultural center as well as the political and administrative capital. The population rose to 3.358 million in 1920 and 7.358 million in 1943. These figures are not all strictly comparable because the administrative boundaries were enlarged in 1932 from 85 square kilometers to 554 square kilometers. Today the area is 2,029 square kilometers.

Tokyo contains the seat of the Emperor, the national legislature, the central government and the highest courts of justice. It is the greatest manufacturing, commercial, and financial center. It has the headquarters of the national newspapers and periodicals, and the publishing, broadcasting and television organs. The leading theatres, both traditional and modern, are situated there. The railway system radiates from Tokyo. It is the center for sport and athletics.

Tokyo University occupies a position of special primacy in higher education, and more than a third of all the colleges and universities in Japan are located there. Tokyo is above all the center of management for all branches of Japanese life. It is, of course, not supreme in every respect. Yokohama is far superior as an ocean port. Osaka and Nagoya excel in some branches of industry.

Tokyo has undergone frequent and severe vicissitudes from fires and earthquakes. Two great disasters occurred in the present century. One was the earthquake of 1923 which caused the death of 74,000 persons and destroyed the homes of two thirds of the survivors. The other was the destruction caused by air raids during the Second World War. About 770,000 houses (roughly half of the total) were destroyed, the devastated area exceeded 39,000 acres, and the sufferers numbered 3 million, including 100,000 killed and 130,000 wounded. The population dropped from over 7 million to 3.5 million in 1945.

Since then it has risen by more than 300,000 a year and has now reached a total in excess of 11 million. This makes Tokyo the world's largest city. The influx was for some years composed of returning soldiers, evacuees and expatriates; but in the last decade more and more people have flocked to the capital in search of employment. Natural increase has also added a substantial element.

No other great city has grown so fast. Moreover, the full extent of its growth is not revealed by the figures set out above because these relate only to the area of the Tokyo metropolitan government. The present administrative boundaries were determined in 1947, and as in the case of most great cities the population has flooded over them.

The modern history of the government of Tokyo dates from 1889 when fifteen wards were incorporated in the City of Tokyo. For nearly a decade the city was administered by a governor of Tokyo prefecture who was appointed by the central government. In 1898 the city council was given the right to elect a mayor but the capital remained under the supervision of the prefectural governor and the minister of home affairs.

In 1943 the prefecture was merged with the city, which then became the Metropolis of Tokyo, combining the powers of a prefecture with those of a city. Numerous wards were added to the original 15 and the number is at present 23. Apart from the special wards the metropolis includes 17 cities, 13 towns and two villages, together with three islands in Tokyo Bay.

Within the special-ward areas, which contain nearly nine million people, Tokyo metropolitan government exercises the major powers of a metropolitan authority. There is a lower tier of elected councils in each of the special wards performing minor functions, but they are subordinate to the Tokyo metropolitan government. Outside the special wards this authority exercises only the powers of a prefecture.

The people of Tokyo have had a long struggle for self-government against the central government. Their greatest victory was in 1947 when the office of governor was made elective by the direct vote of the people. Even today there remains a certain danger of central domination.

Tokyo is the wealthiest city in Japan. The average income per head in the capital is twice the national average and three times as high as in the poor farming districts. The capital contains about 11 percent of the nation and it produces 20 percent of the national income. The Japanese economy has been growing in recent years at a faster rate than that achieved by any other nation at any time, and much of this has been generated in Tokyo, the hub of the economic machine.

The tremendous vitality of the capital is visible on every side. There are new luxury hotels, new theatres, new railway stations, new office blocks, new department stores, the vast stadium and swimming pool built for the Olympic games, new metropolitan freeways, a fast monorail to the airport, the first skyscraper ever permitted in Japan, the new superexpress railway to Osaka running at 200-250 kilometers an hour, and the impressive new managerial subcenter at Shinjuku with vast underground roads, shopping arcades and parking facilities. Motor cars pour off the assembly line at a rate which has placed Japan second among the automobile-producing countries of the world.

Yet below the surface there are serious deficiencies which have not been overcome. The housing situation in Tokyo is bad for the low income groups and it will remain unsatisfactory unless much stronger measures are introduced to restrict profiteering in land. There is a need also for public authorities to provide many more dwellings for the poorer families.

Only 30 percent of the special-ward area has sewerage, and flush toilets are in use in only 27.6 percent of the buildings. A piped water supply is available in 90 percent of the houses in the special-ward area but in three wards the proportion is much lower. Outside the special wards the overall figure is only 64 percent. Moreover, a piped water supply does not imply a regular supply day and night throughout the year.

Public nuisances, such as air pollution, flooding, river pollution, fumes from motor cars, etc. are not effectively controlled. The torrent of motor cars pouring off the assembly lines has produced a traffic problem of immense difficulty, which is exacerbated by an absence of parking meters and an exceptionally low ratio of road space to the metropolitan territory.

The public transport system is grossly overloaded and is divided among public authorities and commercial companies. Its capacity is far below that required to cope with the exceptionally heavy commuter traffic.

In several respects the social development and the basic infrastructure of Tokyo have not kept pace with the increase of population and the growth of the economy.

There are several reasons for this imbalance. The excessively heavy influx of population would have overstrained the resources of any great city. But the huge industrial, commercial and cultural development of Tokyo demanded a much larger investment in public services than has been forthcoming, especially for health, housing, education, public utilities, transport and green spaces.

The central government has failed to provide Tokyo Metropolitan Government with the financial resources and the powers needed to enable it to cope with the pressing problems of the postwar years. Vital matters such as the rocketing price of land, the planning of the Tokyo region, the expansion of the city boundaries, the development of countermagnets in other parts of the country, a more generous system of subsidies and loans for municipal purposes, have either been neglected or dealt with ineffectively.

Despite its problems, Tokyo represents a massive achievement by any standard. It is a modern city embodying many feats of design, technology and construction which are highly esteemed in the modern world. It must be compared, not with the squalid and poverty-stricken cities of Asia but with the centers of wealth, fashion and luxury of Western Europe and North America.

And it contains within itself that fascinating and unique feature of Japanese society: the dual culture. One sees the technical perfection of the Tokaido express railway, the marvels of modern radio and television factories, the ingenious design of the latest department store building, the Festival Concert Hall, a highly accomplished national press, the stainless steel station at Shinjuku, a splendid exhibition of Utrillo's paintings, and many other manifestations of Western science and art.

One also sees the No theatre and the Kabuki, the ancient Shinto shrines and Buddhist temples, the kimonos and the traditional wedding costumes, the lovely gardens, the incense-burning ceremonies, the tea ceremony, the flower-arranging art, the Japanese-style houses, rooms and customs which have persisted through long centuries. [See "Facts about Japan" in this section, below, for an explanation of some of these cultural features.—Ed.]

Nowhere else can one see ancient and modern cultures coexisting in this way without merging. The result is a triumph for what has been achieved since the Meiji Restoration. It is also a tribute to what was achieved before that important event.

FACTS ABOUT JAPAN [4]

Religion

The three major religions in Japan are Shinto, Buddhism and Christianity. The first is indigenous and the others were introduced from abroad, Buddhism in the sixth century and Christianity in the sixteenth. Besides these major religions, many forms of religious belief exist in Japan.

[4] From publication of the Public Information Bureau, Ministry of Foreign Affairs, Government of Japan. The Bureau. Tokyo. '69.

Confucianism has had a considerable bearing on the formation of the Japanese national character, but its influence has declined in recent years....

Shinto. Shinto, an indigenous ancestor worship, has its origin in the ancient traditions connected with ancestral gods. It has no codified doctrine or creed of any kind other than worship offered to the Imperial ancestors and the ancestral spirits. A Shinto shrine is a place of worship dedicated to a guardian deity whose spirit is symbolized usually by a metal mirror placed on the altar.

Because . . . [Shinto is] intertwined with the mythology of the origin of the nation, it was the religion most closely connected with the government in Japan. There were times when the government in . . . [Japan] took on the appearance of a theocracy.

Shinto was formerly of two types, namely National Shinto or Shrine Shinto and Sectarian Shinto which developed toward the end of the Tokugawa Shogunate (1603-1867).

In 1868, immediately after the Meiji Restoration, the government established a Shinto Office and designated Shrine Shinto as a national institution, simultaneously giving a privileged status to all Shinto Shrines, but under the constitution of 1947, Shinto was reduced to the same status as all other religious institutions....

Buddhism. Buddhism came to Japan from India through China and Korea in 538 A.D. Prince Shotoku, Regent from 593 to 628 A.D., was largely responsible for its rapid spread throughout the country. Six schools of Buddhism—Sanron, Hosso, Jojitsu, Kusha, Ritsu, and Kegon—were introduced one after the other.

In the reign of Emperor Kammu (782-805 A.D.), Tendai and Shingon flourished. New schools such as Jodo, Zen, Shin, Nichiren and others then gradually developed. The principal sects still in existence are Hosso, Kegon, Ritsu, Tendai, Shingon, Yuzunembutsu, Jodo, Shin, Ji, Zen and Nichiren, and these eleven are subdivided into fifty-eight branches.

Buddhism has long occupied the most important place in the religious life of Japan. It had a great influence on the fine arts and on social institutions and customs, and greatly contributed to the promotion of learning and the arts.

Christianity. Christianity was first introduced to Japan by St. Francis Xavier, a Jesuit Father, when he came to Kyushu in 1549. It spread quite rapidly at first with the encouragement of some feudal lords. In the latter half of the sixteenth century, however, Christianity was outlawed. It was not until the middle of the nineteenth century, when Japan opened its doors to foreign nations, that Christianity returned. Christians, both foreign missionaries and Japanese, became very active and the number of believers has steadily increased. The Bible was first printed in Japan in 1887 and complete religious freedom was given to all Christians in 1889.

Christianity was regarded as representing Western civilization in the modernization of all spheres of life in Japan after the Meiji Restoration. Christian churches in Japan followed the historic divisions of the West into Roman Catholic, Eastern Orthodox and the various Protestant churches.

Kabuki

Kabuki is one of Japan's traditional theatrical arts. Its inception goes back to the latter part of the sixteenth century and, with extensive and continuous evolution, it has now been perfected into a state of classical refinement. Though not as flourishing as it once was, the Kabuki theatre retains a wide popularity among the people, and is in fact drawing quite large audiences even now.

During the period generally referred to as the Yedo Era, during which much of the development of Kabuki took place, distinction between the warrior class and the commoners was more rigidly observed than at any other time in Japan's history. The art of Kabuki was cultivated mainly by the merchants in those days. They had become increasingly powerful economically, but had to remain socially inferior as they belonged to the commoner class. To them Kabuki was perhaps most significant as the artistic means by which to express their emotions under such conditions. Thus, the fundamental themes of Kabuki plays are conflicts between humanity and the feudalistic system. It is largely due to this humanistic quality of the art that it gained such an enduring popularity among the general public of those days and remains this way today.

A unique feature of the Kabuki art, and perhaps the most significant and in keeping with the Kabuki spirit of unusualness, is the fact that it has no actresses whatsoever. All female parts are played by male impersonators known as *onnagata*. The players of the Kabuki drama in its primitive stage were principally women, and with the increasing popularity of Kabuki, many of the actresses began to attract undue attention from male admirers. The authorities felt that this would lead to a serious demoralization of the public and in 1629 the theatrical appearance of women was officially banned.

However, since Kabuki as an art form was already accepted by the public, men immediately took over and have continued performing to the present. The ban on actresses was in effect for about 250 years. In the meantime Kabuki brought to perfection the art of the *onnagata*. As a result, there was no room for actresses in Kabuki when the ban was lifted. Moreover, the art of *onnagata* had become such an integral part of Kabuki that, if deprived of this element, the traditional quality of Kabuki could be lost forever.

Another important characteristic of Kabuki is that it is an inclusive and accumulative theatre. Born at the turn of the sixteenth century, it incorporated parts of all the preceding theatre forms of Japan. Among the traditional arts from which Kabuki has drawn for stage techniques and repertoire are the No drama [classic, and heroic in subject] and the Kyogen play, or the comic interlude presented between No performances. Today, the number of Japanese who appreciate No proper is far smaller than that of those who favor Kabuki, but those Kabuki plays adapted from or inspired by No plays enjoy a wide popularity and constitute an essential portion of the entire Kabuki repertoire.

Another area from which Kabuki has borrowed is the puppet theatre, often referred to as Bunraku, the development of which roughly paralleled that of earlier Kabuki. In Kabuki, the primary importance has always been placed on the actor rather than on any other aspect of the art, such as literary value of a play. During the early seventeenth century, some of the great writers . . . left Kabuki with its actors' domination and turned to the puppet theatre where their creative genius was more or less unrestricted. As a result, there was a period when puppets overshadowed actors and the puppet theatre was more popular than Kabuki. To meet this competition, Kabuki adopted virtually all the puppet plays. Thus, today more than half of the conventional Kabuki plays except for a group of dance-dramas are of Bunraku origin. A final example of Kabuki's all-embracing acquisitiveness came at the end of the nineteenth century, which added an element of literary realism to the art.

Until Kabuki, the people of Japan had never seen theatre of such color, glamor, excitement and general extraordinariness. In these qualities, perhaps no theatre elsewhere in the world can excel the Kabuki drama.

Bunraku

Puppet shows have existed since olden times in almost all countries of the world. In most of their forms, the puppet is manipulated either directly by hand (guignols) or by strings and wires (marionettes), while in some shadows of puppets are used. The plots often cater to juvenile audiences.

The Japanese puppet show, known as Bunraku, in which each puppet is operated by three men, requires a superior degree of skill in manipulation and features elaborate forms of expression and superb artistry. In these respects, Bunraku is a precious heritage of folk culture in which Japan can take a justifiable pride.

Bunraku consists of three human elements: the Tayu who recites the Joruri, which is a poetic form something like an epical drama; the Shamisen player who, with the three-stringed instrument, provides musical accompaniment for the recitation; and the puppet manipulator. In other words, the story narrated by the Tayu is an epical poem written in a certain dramatic form, the Shamisen, while accompanying the narration, creates a musical atmosphere for the play, and the puppets are made to perform in accordance with the chanting and musical accompaniment, producing a combined effect not unlike an operatic presentation.

The puppets used in a Bunraku performance usually range in height from three to four-and-a-half feet. They are manipulated by three men, although those used for bit parts are operated by only one or two.

Each puppet is made up of a wooden head, trunk, arms and legs; each of the component parts can be detached from the others. The head is steadied on the trunk by inserting the rod on the bottom of the neck into the hole in the center of the wooden Kata-ita (shoulder plate), which corresponds anatomically to the collarbones. The costume is placed over the shoulder plate and the trunk, which has bamboo hoops attached to it to form the hips. The arms and legs are hung from the shoulder plate with strings. The rod under the head has strings to move the eyes, mouth and eyebrows. . . .

The leading manipulator, Omo-zukai, inserts his left hand into the hole in the hip and holds the neck rod between his right thumb and index finger. While thus supporting the weight of the puppet, he uses the remaining three right fingers to manipulate the strings to move the eyes, mouth and eyebrows. His right hand is used for moving the puppet's right arm.

Supporting the puppet is no easy task. Even a light female puppet weighs about . . . [13 pounds] and a fully armored warrior can weigh as much as . . . [44 pounds]. With this heavy load on his left arm, the Omo-zukai performs over long periods of time.

The puppet's left arm is operated by the Hidari-zukai, who plays an assisting role. He must work in perfect co-ordination with the Omo-zukai, constantly watching the direction of the puppet's head and accordingly determining the position of the left arm.

The legs of the puppet are operated by the Ashi-zukai, who moves the L-shaped hooks attached to the back of the puppet's heels back and forth or left to right to imitate the motion of legs. The Ashi-zukai's work is most fatiguing be-cause all the while he must remain hidden from the audience by assuming a stooping posture.

Since three persons handle the different parts of a puppet, lifelike motion cannot be expected without precision timing among the three. For all motions, there are detailed rules and forms to be followed; no manipulator is allowed to act on his own. Besides realistic performances faithfully copying human carriage and deportment, there are forms of motion unique to Bunraku. They are at once exaggerated and clever-ly stylized.

When operating the puppets on stage, the manipulators as a rule wear black gowns (known as Kurogo) and black hoods. This is because dressing in black signifies that the puppet is the main performer with the manipulator remain-ing behind the scene. In the Japanese theatrical tradition, there is a rule that the black costume represents something invisible, or nothingness.

Chanoyu—Tea Ceremony

The tea ceremony, referred to as *chanoyu* in Japan, is an esthetic pastime peculiar to Japan that features the serving and drinking of *matcha*, a powdered green tea.

According to recorded history, tea was introduced into Japan around 700 A.D. from China. . . . *Matcha,* as used in the tea ceremony today, was still unknown at the time. It was not until toward the end of the twelfth century that *matcha* was brought into Japan from China of the Sung dynasty. However, tea was still very precious and was used mostly as a medicine rather than as a beverage. Tea drinking was practiced almost exclusively among Zen Buddhist priests who used it to prevent drowsiness during their long hours of meditation.

The popularization of tea began early in the fourteenth century, when a game called *tocha* (tea contest) was introduced from China. This was a party diversion in which the guests, being served several cups of tea produced in different regions, were called upon to select the one containing the tea produced in the best tea-growing area. Those who guessed correctly were given prizes. As this game came into vogue, tea plantations began to flourish, especially in the Uji district near Kyoto, where tea of the best quality is still produced.

The *tocha* was gradually converted into a more sedate social gathering, at which prizes were no longer awarded, so as better to suit the tastes of the Japanese people. The aim now became the enjoyment of a profound atmosphere in which the tea was served. At the same time, under the influence of formalities regulating the everyday life of the *Samurai*, or warriors, who were then the dominant class of the country, there came into being certain rules and procedures which the participants in a tea party were required to obey.

It was a man named Murata Juko (1423-1502) who, out of this tradition, created the fundamentals of ceremonial tea drinking known as *chanoyu*. His legacy was inherited by, among others, Takeno Jo-o (1502-1555), who set forth the principles of *chanoyu*, taught by Juko, in more concrete terms. A Zen priest by the name of Sen Rikyu (1521-1591) finally perfected *chanoyu* to its present form.

Chanoyu, thus developed, is something more than a refined form of taking refreshment. Its purpose and essence are difficult to express in words. It will be helpful to remember that the ceremony was developed under the influence of

Zen Buddhism, the aim of which is, in simple terms, to purify one's soul by becoming one with nature. In addition, *chanoyu* is an embodiment of the Japanese people's intuitive striving for recognition of true beauty in plainness and simplicity. Such terms as calmness, rusticity, gracefulness, or the phrase "estheticism of austere simplicity and refined poverty," may help to define the true spirit of *chanoyu*. For instance, the strict canons of *chanoyu* etiquette, which may seem to be burdensome and meticulous at first glance, are in fact minutely calculated to achieve the highest possible economy of movement and indeed is pleasing for the initiated to witness, especially when performed by experienced masters.

Chanoyu has played an important role in the artistic life of the Japanese people, since, as an esthetic pursuit, it involves the appreciation of the room in which it is held, the garden attached to the room, the utensils used in serving the tea, and the decor of the setting, such as a hanging scroll or an *ikebana* (flower arrangement). The development of Japan's architecture, landscape gardening, ceramics and the floral arts, therefore, owes a great deal to the tea ceremony. It should be noted that, throughout all these and other artistic elements connected with *chanoyu*, there prevails that love of simplicity which is characteristic of the Japanese people.

Furthermore, the development of daily manners of the majority of the Japanese have been basically influenced by formalities such as those observed in the *chanoyu* ceremony. As a result, it is a rather common practice for young ladies before marriage to take lessons in the art in order to cultivate the poise and refinement stemming from *chanoyu* etiquette.

II. JAPAN YESTERDAY AND TODAY

EDITOR'S INTRODUCTION

The pendulum of Japanese history has swung wildly in this century. The first decade of the century saw a Japanese fleet destroying the Russian navy. In World War I, Japan sided with the Allies. In World War II, it was one of the Axis powers and, with them, suffered a crushing defeat. After the war, Japan was occupied by American troops. In the postwar decades Japan reconstructed itself, modernized its society, and became a staunch friend of the United States, on which it depended for military security. This section reviews some of the changes that have occurred and puts them in the context of Japanese cultural and social patterns so as to outline broad characteristics and problems of Japanese society today.

The first article, taken from a Foreign Policy Association publication, describes the historical setting and illustrates how the reforms instituted by the United States after the war stimulated the progress which has resulted in the emergence of Japan as a major Pacific and world power. The next selection relates the economic boom to the values and characteristics of the society. This analysis illustrates the traits the Japanese people have long cultivated and shows how these characteristics must be appreciated if we are to understand Japan today. The article ends with a quotation from a Japanese executive. "Business is my hobby," he says, and that seems to explain much.

The following article looks beyond the economic boom to assess the social costs to Japan of its material prosperity. For one thing, prosperity is unevenly distributed. For another, inflation and a relative lack of some of the necessary municipal services plague urban dwellers.

The last selection, taken from an address by Prime Minister Eisaku Sato, dwells on what he calls "discontinuity." This refers to the fact that while Japan is in most respects a thoroughly modern society, it is plagued with problems that reflect the clash between the demands of an industrial environment and traditional spiritual and moral values. It is essential, the prime minister states, for Japan to overcome this discontinuity.

THE GEOGRAPHICAL AND HISTORICAL SETTING [1]

Is Japan an Asian country? It is easier to ask the question than to answer it. A glance at the map shows that geographically the four main islands—Hokkaido, Honshu, Shikoku and Kyushu—form a 1,500-mile crescent off the coast of Northeast Asia. South and North Korea, Communist China and the Soviet far east are physically Japan's closest neighbors. Racially, the 103.5 million Japanese are akin to the Chinese and Koreans. Geographically and ethnically, then, Japan and the Japanese would seem to be Asian.

Economically and politically, however, the Japanese today are much closer to North America and Western Europe than to their neighbors on the Asian continent. The Japanese economy is the third most productive in the world. Japan leads in shipbuilding, is second in computers and automobile output, and third in steel production and electric power capacity. The Japanese standard of living is comparable in most respects to that in Western Europe. More than half of Japan's foreign trade is with the United States, Canada, Australia, Latin America and Western Europe. Communist China and the Soviet Union together account for only 4 percent of Japan's trade. Moreover, technologically, Japanese ties with the developed, non-Communist world

[1] From *Japan—The Risen Sun*, pamphlet by Martin E. Weinstein, assistant professor of political science, University of Illinois. (Headline Series No. 202) Foreign Policy Association. 345 E. 46th St. New York 10017. '70. p 3-15. Reprinted with permission from Headline Series #202. Copyright 1970 by the Foreign Policy Association, Inc.

are even closer than the trade figures suggest. Politically, Japan is a constitutional monarchy ruled by a parliamentary-cabinet form of government modeled on a mixture of the American and British systems. And since World War II, the Japanese government has based its foreign and defense policies on close cooperation with the United States.

It is well to keep this incongruity between Japan's geographical and cultural locations in mind, because it poses an identity problem for the Japanese. They are, at times, unsure themselves whether they are Asian, Western or something other; a composite of tradition and modernity, as their travel posters claim; or, as one Japanese sociologist has argued, a postmodern society. Moreover, this incongruity also baffles the foreigner trying to understand Japan. The Tokyo traffic jams, the Osaka smog, the color TV and the student violence all incline the observer to describe and analyze the Japanese in the same terms and with the same categories as he would use to describe and analyze the Americans or the French. But when he has looked more closely at the Japanese, has seen how they run their factories, study in their schools and relax at home, the foreign observer usually decides that his terms and categories do not quite fit. From that realization some have jumped to the extreme conclusion that beneath their computers, their high quality steel and their stock market, the Japanese are a people whose values and behavior have remained basically insular and unchanged since feudal times despite industrialization and extended, sometimes violent, contact with the outside world.

Japan's Modernization: Phase I

Historically, Japan's identity problem can be traced back to the last three decades of the nineteenth century. From about 1870 until World War I an outstanding group of talented energetic leaders, known as the Meiji oligarchs, or Genro, made a conscious effort to transform their politically fragmented land of rice farmers into a centralized, industrialized state modeled on European lines. [See "Emperor

Meiji—Father of Modern Japan," in Section I, above, for a detailed account of these reforms.—Ed.] Their goal was to build Japan into a state strong enough to defend itself and to compete in international affairs with the then leading Western powers—Britain, France, Germany, Russia and the United States. During that period, the exploitation and humiliation of China led the Japanese to denigrate their traditional values and ideals, many of which had come to them from China, and to throw themselves feverishly into the effort to westernize. This initial effort probably reached its high-water mark in the Russo-Japanese War of 1904-05. In that war the Japanese fleet, largely built in Japan, destroyed the Russian navy, and following the surrender of the Russian army at Port Arthur, General Nogi gallantly returned the sword tendered him by the defeated Russian commander. In military might, as in etiquette, the Japanese were ready to join the "society of civilized nations." They were ready to carry the gifts of technology and orderly government to their recently conquered Korean and Taiwanese colonies and even to the Chinese. They looked forward to reaping the benefits of commercial equality in a world of fast-growing trade. And they anticipated the prestige of diplomatic parity with the great powers.

Phase 2: Reaction Against the West

It is doubtful, however, that the Japanese ever felt completely accepted by the great powers. Despite the assurances offered by Britain in the Anglo-Japanese alliance of 1902 and its renewal in both 1905 and 1911, and despite a widespread admiration and respect in the West for Japanese energy and aggressiveness, there continued to be slights to Japan's dignity. Perhaps the most galling of these were the restrictions imposed on Japanese immigration by the United States, Canada and Australia. Even more to the point, the horrors and destruction of World War I, during which Japan sided with the Allies, raised the question of whether there

was indeed a society of "civilized nations" to which Japan
could or ought to belong.

During the 1920s, Japan's leaders smothered their doubts
and did their best to help put the old world, that had been
so promising, back together again. In the 1930s, however, the
world depression and the rise of [trade] protectionism . . .
[and] fascism in Italy and Nazism in Germany—all convinced
them that a society of civilized nations no longer existed.
Japan's leaders came to believe that their country's economic
and military security lay in an East Asian coprosperity sphere.
It was to be Asia for the Asians. Japanese military forces
would organize and protect the region from further depre-
dations by the white, Western colonial powers. Although
Japan continued to industrialize during the 1930s, the Japanese were self-consciously turning away from the West. The
West was no longer respected and emulated. Being a good
Japanese came to mean cultivating a traditional, Oriental
spirit, a spirit that defied precise definition but was nevertheless believed to be superior to the corrupt, materialist
values of the liberal West.

Along with this pronounced psychological reaction
against the West, the 1930s also witnessed the breakdown of
constitutional government. During the rapid Westernization
phase of the late nineteenth century, the Meiji leaders had
built a constitutional monarchy similar in form to that of
pre-World War I Germany. There was an elected Diet
[parliament] but its powers were sharply limited. The prime
minister and cabinet were legally appointed by the emperor
and responsible to him, not to the Diet. In practice, however, the emperor only acted on the behest of his advisers.
While the Meiji oligarchs were alive and active—until World
War I—they were the emperor's advisers. They provided the
nucleus of centralized, coordinated government by their
dominant positions in the court, the army and navy, the
civilian bureaucracy and the political parties. During the
1920s, following the oligarchy's demise, the military services
suffered a decline in size and political influence. The politi-

cal parties, with the cooperation of the court and civilian bureaucrats, moved toward a representative, responsible cabinet form of government.

With the collapse of world economic and political order in the 1930s, however, the military leaders, by exploiting and reinforcing the pervading insecurity and xenophobia, greatly strengthened their political position. Before the end of the decade they dominated the government. The army and navy leaders stood for forceful expansion abroad and military discipline and organization at home; for a religious reverence for the emperor, in whose name they were acting; and for the belief that Japan, as the leader of Asia, enjoyed a unique, spiritual superiority.

It was in this frame of mind, and under this military influence, that the Japanese invaded Manchuria in 1931, left the League of Nations in 1933 and became involved in 1937 in a seemingly endless war against the Chinese, who did not want Japanese leadership and protection. And it was in search of the goal of regional hegemony in East Asia that the Japanese attacked and destroyed the American fleet at Pearl Harbor in 1941 and in so doing widened the European war [which had begun in 1939] into a second world war.

Phase 3: Legacy of the Occupation

When the Japanese surrendered to the Allies in September 1945, they did more than end World War II. They also closed this confused, contradictory second phase in their modern era. Their unprecedented and humiliating military defeat demonstrated the inadequacy of the institutions, the leaders and the values which had led them into the war. The presence of foreign troops in the country, the bombed-out cities, the terrible shortages of food and clothing, were taken as proof by most people of the failure of the old and traditional and of the necessity of building a new, different Japan. But defeat not only produced a willingness to experiment. It also produced bewilderment, dread and apathy. The devastation of the war had been so great, and the task of rebuilding the country was so vast. Who were to be Japan's new leaders? Within what institutions were they to operate? And most important of all, What values and goals were to get the Japanese back to work, putting together their country and their own dislocated lives?

We can hardly conceive the physical and psychological damage suffered by the Japanese between 1944 and 1946. The moral uncertainty and confusion in the United States resulting from a limited war in Vietnam that seemingly cannot be won barely hints at the consequences of a total war that had been utterly lost.

In retrospect, it appears an extraordinary coincidence that the Americans, who had bitterly fought the Japanese from one island to the next across the breadth of the Pacific, had constructive answers to these questions. The Americans, too, were convinced that it was necessary to build a new, different Japan, and they arrived full of energy and ideas. During the war, plans had been made in Washington for an Allied occupation which would transform what were believed to be the militaristic, authoritarian Japanese into a peace-loving, democratic people. Thousands of Americans had been trained in the Japanese language and given courses in Japanese history and institutions. They felt ready to undertake the most ambitious job of social engineering ever attempted. We can see today that the "occupationnaires" had their share of misconceptions and made mistakes. The Japanese were not as authoritarian and militaristic as the occupation planners assumed they were. But we can also see that they went to Japan not simply as conquerors intent on punishment but as reformers, intent on rehabilitating the recent enemy. The Japanese quickly perceived this. Instead of treating the occupation with bitter, truculent defiance, they welcomed its enthusiasm and sense of direction. To an extraordinary degree, the Japanese were willing to tolerate its misconceptions, suffer its mistakes and make the best of its reforms.

From Defeated Enemy to Ally

Unlike Germany, Japan was not divided into zones of occupation and was never ruled directly by occupying armies. Instead, the country was placed under the control of the Supreme Commander for the Allied Powers (SCAP), General Douglas MacArthur, who conducted the occupation through the Japanese government. In effect, despite Japan's theoretically unconditional surrender, SCAP's authority could only be effective to the extent that the Japanese accepted it. General MacArthur recognized from the beginning that the success of the occupation would depend on Japanese cooperation.

In order to get that cooperation, he treated the recently defeated enemy with magnanimity and respect, even when doing so involved resistance to directives from Washington, where officials were inclined to be more vindictive toward Japan than General MacArthur deemed necessary or wise. General MacArthur's insistence on relying on his own judgment, even when it ran counter to official orders, was eventually to lead to his dismissal by President Harry S. Truman in 1951, during the Korean war. However, his chivalrous treatment of the Japanese in the anxious, uncertain winter of 1945-46, when chivalry ran counter to United States policy, was an indispensable contribution to the success of the occupation. By 1948, this philosophy permitted the occupation to become a joint Japanese-American venture. And by 1952, when the occupation ended and Japan regained its independence in the midst of the Korean war, there was little doubt that Japan and the United States would continue their close political, military and economic ties and would be allies in the cold war.

In Japan, critics of the government's foreign policy have insistently argued that the United States-Japanese security treaties of 1951 and 1960 were imposed on an unwilling Japan and that American bases in the country constitute continuation of the occupation. One does not have to agree with this criticism to recognize that it contains a kernel of truth. Japan's [current] posture in international affairs is . . . indeed a legacy of its defeat and occupation. But it should also be recognized that if our occupation had been vindictive and punitive, if it had not been motivated by a determination to rebuild Japan along lines acceptable to most Japanese, Japan and the United States would not have been able to cooperate as they have since 1952, and we would not be allies today.

Internal Reforms

Japan's domestic institutions were as much affected by the occupation as its external relations, and the domestic changes may prove to be longer lasting. As conceived in Washington before the surrender, the broad aims of the occupation were to be "demilitarization and democratization." In the immediate aftermath of the war, demilitarization naturally had first priority. By early 1946, Japan's armed forces, which were over five million strong at the surrender, had virtually all been repatriated, disarmed and demobilized. The imperial army and navy ministries, which had played such powerful roles in prewar politics, were abolished. The highest ranking former officers, as well as prominent civilians who had worked with the military, were temporarily banned from public life.

The Japanese accepted the demilitarization program and implemented much of it themselves. Following the fire bombing of Tokyo, Osaka and Nagoya and the horrors of Hiroshima and Nagasaki, they had had their bellyful of war and military establishments. The military leaders, led by General and former Prime Minister Hideki Tojo, took full responsibility for their defeat. They stoically suffered its consequences, even when it entailed their own executions as war criminals. Finally, the demilitarization program was institutionalized in Article 9 of the occupation-sponsored Constitution, which came into effect in 1947. According to Article 9:

Aspiring sincerely to an international peace based on justice and order, the Japanese people forever renounce war as a sovereign right of the nation and the threat or use of force as means of settling international disputes.

In order to accomplish the aim of the preceding paragraph, land, sea and air forces, as well as other war potential, will never be maintained. The right of belligerency of the state will not be recognized.

. . . Since 1950, Japan has built limited, conventionally armed self-defense forces, which, it has been argued, are in direct violation of Article 9. It should be noted here, however, that the questionable constitutionality of these forces, along with the present impotence of military officers in Japanese politics, are themselves direct products of the occupation's demilitarization program.

After destroying the military class and institutions, which had been predominant in the prewar government, the occupation proceeded with its democratization program to further modify Japan's political institutions. The 1947 constitution did not abolish the emperor, but it did divest his office of all political powers and reduced it to a symbol of the state. Sovereignty was vested in the people. The prewar, bicameral legislature, known as the Diet, was greatly strengthened and assigned the major role in the new government. The prime minister would be elected in the Diet and he and his cabinet would be responsible to the Diet. An independent judiciary was created, and the Japanese people were guaranteed all the civil rights necessary to an open, free society. As we have seen, the Japanese had started to construct a parliamentary democracy in the 1920s. The occupation's political reforms were not entirely novel. But they went much further toward an egalitarian society than the 1920 liberals had dreamed of going.

The occupation saw to it that this new structure was staffed and led by men who favored constitutional, parliamentary government. And here again, fortune favored the Americans and the Japanese. These leaders were neither servile nor incompetent. Most of the men who took charge of the new institutions were highly intelligent, independent and patriotically Japanese. Outstanding among them were Kijuro Shidehara, who had been foreign minister in the 1920s, and Shigeru Yoshida, also a former diplomat, who was to head the government almost continuously from 1946 to 1954. . . .

It is appropriate to note here that under the new occupation-sponsored constitution, to get political power it is necessary to be elected to the Diet. Strengthening the Diet has served to strengthen the political parties, which had been of only peripheral importance in prewar Japan. Moreover, quite early in the occupation, businessmen and to a lesser extent labor unions became the principal sources of the funds necessary to maintain the parties and to finance election campaigns. Thus, by the time Japan regained its full sovereignty in 1952, the constitutional, parliamentary, cabinet form of government, which operates today, was solidly formed. The bureaucracy, the political parties and the sources of political funds had all taken shape. . . .

Despite SCAP's initial plans, Japanese economic life was less dramatically altered than was intended. Between 1945 and 1948, the occupation pursued a *zaibatsu* dissolution policy, i.e., one aimed at breaking down the huge financial-industrial combines which had provided the economic base for Japan's military power. By 1948, however, two factors led SCAP to a change of heart. First, during 1946 and 1947, General MacArthur came to the conclusion that his political reforms were not going to take hold unless the Japanese people were given a reasonably stable, secure livelihood. Second, his concern over economic recovery was reinforced by the United States—Soviet cold war hostility and by the course of the civil war in China. In brief, by 1948 we were beginning to see Japan as a potential ally, and we wanted our ally to be economically sound. It had become evident that a Japanese industrial economy composed exclusively of small and medium enterprises was unworkable. The zaibatsu managers knew how to run large, efficient firms. SCAP decided to work with them.

By the time SCAP decided to let the zaibatsu-type business organizations survive, however, it had basically altered the social and political environment in which they would have to live. In particular, with the occupation's guidance and encouragement, Japanese labor was organized into powerful unions that were protected by law and the constitution. The revived zaibatsu would have to come to terms with organized labor and meet many of its demands.

In the agricultural sector, SCAP's influence was more decisive. Under the occupation, Japan underwent a thorough land redistribution. In 1945 approximately 47 percent of the land was being worked by tenant farmers. When the occupation ended, close to 90 percent of the arable land was owned by the people cultivating it. The political effect of the land reform was to make the countryside a satisfied, conservative stronghold. Economically and socially, the farmer's lot was dramatically improved. However, the opportunities presented by Japan's burgeoning industries were nevertheless to attract the farmer's children to the cities. Today, despite improved conditions, the farms are short-handed, and the shift of population to the cities is reducing the importance of the rural vote.

Finally, the occupation not only reformed Japan's political and economic life and fostered a new class of leaders. It also attempted to give the Japanese a new set of values to replace those lost in the war and defeat. In a broad sense, these new values were implicit in the demilitarization and democratization programs. Imperial glory, military might and unquestioning obedience to tradition and established authority were to be replaced by pacifism, the rights and well-being of the individual and an open, inquisitive, critical spirit.

It was generally believed that the Japanese had imbibed their prewar militarism and ultranationalism in the schools. It was in the schools, therefore, that the new democratic values would have to take root and be preserved. Consequently, SCAP undertook a thorough revision of the educational organization and curriculum, from the nursery schools right through to the postgraduate divisions of the universities. The occupation's educational reforms, by striking at the very roots of Japanese culture and values, were in many ways its most ambitious. As one might expect, however, their results are most difficult to determine. There is no doubt that pacifism has been a central tenet of postwar education. So much so that most of the postwar generation finds it difficult to deal rationally with a world in which armed force and violence play a large role. Democracy, as expressed in individual liberties and freedom of thought and expression, also seems to have been firmly imprinted on the minds of the young. It is not so certain that the less exciting virtues of representative government and parliamentary politics have come across with the same strength and clarity. Moreover, despite its reorganization and revised ideology, the style of the educators is less changed than that of the political and business communities. Many Japanese teachers tend to be as doctrinaire as their prewar predecessors. It often appears that they are as blindly dedicated to preserving Article 9 of the peace Constitution as prewar teachers were to preserving the imperial institution.

Summing up—during the last century the Japanese experience has been unlike that of any other people in Asia. Between 1870 and 1900, they successfully molded themselves into a centralized, industrialized state with powerful military forces. By doing so, they managed to escape the humiliation of colonization and foreign exploitation. In this century they participated in world politics as a major power, but failed catastrophically in an effort to become the undisputed military, political and economic leader of East Asia. Following their defeat in World War II, the Japanese cooperated with the American occupation in dramatically reforming their country. Most Americans have forgotten the occupation. The Japanese, however, live very much with the results, perhaps too much so. And now, after twenty-five years of hard work and quiet diplomacy, Japan is again a major power, alone in Asia in enjoying great prosperity and a relatively high degree of political stability under a parliamentary, democratic government.

CULTURE AND THE BOOM [2]

The [Japanese] economy is an expression of a society that values order, security, harmony and industry. Japan has become the world exemplar of what in the West is called the Protestant ethic. The reasons behind Japan's work ethic lie not in its Buddhist and Shinto religions but in its history and geography. The mountainous nation has always been a tough place to scratch out a living. The peasant who did not labor hard simply starved, partly because medieval lords took as much as 80 percent of his rice crop in taxes. Necessity was transmuted into virtue: the busy man is a good man. To this day, it is considered respectful to greet superiors by saying, *"O-isogashii desho* [You must be in an honorably busy state of affairs]."

Single-minded dedication to a goal is easier to achieve in Japan than in the West because Japan is the largest homogeneous society on earth: there are only tiny racial or even linguistic minorities among its 104 million people. Harmony and order are also essential because the Japanese have always been jammed together on small patches of arable land. The physical proximity of the Japanese breeds tension, which can be discharged by hard work, but there is literally no room for aggressively individualistic behavior. There is a violent undercurrent that sometimes leads to street demonstrations or parliamentary brawls, and the Japanese struggle to contain it. . . .

Western executives are often perplexed and sometimes misled by the extreme reluctance of the courteous Japanese

[2] From "Japan, Inc.: Winning the Most Important Battle." *Time* 97:46-8. My. 10, '71. Reprinted by permission from *Time*, The Weekly Newsmagazine; copyright Time Inc., 1971.

to answer any suggestion with a flat no. Japanese are equally shocked by Western bluntness. Yoshio Terazawa, executive vice president of US operations for Nomura Securities, a giant brokerage house, recalls the dismay of a colleague who watched an American lawyer spend hours haggling over the fine print of a contract. In Japan, such matters would be settled by gentlemen's agreement.

Another element in Japan's economic psychology is its long history of cultural isolation. When the nation was finally opened to the West a century ago, the Japanese felt a morbid fear that they were behind the rest of the world and a compulsive drive to catch up. In that drive, the World War II defeat and the US occupation turned into a major plus. Occupation authorities purged the old, politically oriented heads of Japanese businesses, replacing them with well-trained technicians who had learned many lessons during the war. (Today's superb Japanese camera lenses, for example, are the end result of wartime research into range finders.)

Advantages of Being in Hock

Forbidden by the American-imposed constitution to buy modern weaponry, Japan has been able to concentrate investment on automated industry. The destruction of its factories by wartime bombing left it free to rebuild with the latest technology. To do that quickly, the new industrialists bought patents and licenses from everywhere. Says Shigeo Nagano, chairman of Nippon Steel, which today produces more tonnage than any other company in the world: "So long as we had to start from nothing, we wanted the most modern plant. We selected the cream of the world's technology. We learned from America, Germany, Austria and the Soviet Union, and adapted their methods in our own way." In particular, the Japanese developed a strategy of looking for "technological gaps"—advances that were not being fully exploited in the West. The oxygen steel·.aking process, for example, was developed in Austria, bu'. Nagano and his colleagues were quicker to appreciate its quality and cost-saving features than their Western rivals were. More than 80 percent of Japan's steel is now made in oxygen furnaces, the highest proportion in the world.

Faced with a severe postwar capital famine, all industry had to borrow heavily from government-regulated banks. Even today, Japanese companies generally get more than 80 percent of their financing from loans and less than 20 percent from sale of stock—about the opposite of the ratio in the US. Nagano estimates that Nippon Steel's debt is equal to what four or five American steel companies would owe. To a Western executive that might seem to leave the economy extremely vulnerable to a Penn Central-type collapse. Japanese find that being in hock has its advantages: corporate pooh-bahs do not have to worry about paying high dividends or showing plump profits to keep stockholders happy.

To a large extent the Japanese worker has financed this system. His phenomenal savings rate, a product of the desire for security, has fed funds to the industrial machine. Last year [1970] the Japanese saved 19.4 percent of their incomes; in the United States, a 7 percent savings rate is considered startlingly high. . . .

The Charm of the Company Union

In order to help industry produce inexpensively and expand quickly, workers long had to accept low wages. In return, they received an implied guarantee of lifetime jobs in the companies that they joined fresh out of school. That security has bred one of the world's most contented work forces. Japanese workers rarely strike, and absenteeism is almost unknown. Unions lately have become more vocal. Wages climbed an average 18 percent last year—but, incredibly, productivity rose 14 percent. Japan's average wages, now 94 cents an hour, passed Italy's in 1969 and France's . . . [in 1970].

One reason that productivity is soaring is that unions have not resisted new technology. If a man's skill becomes obsolete, his company retrains him for something else, with no loss in pay. Employers thus have great freedom to shift workers from one job to another and can invest huge sums to train them without worrying that they will jump to competing firms. As a result, workers tend to identify with the company rather than with a particular skill, a fact that is reflected in union organization. Says . . . [one Japanese executive], smiling: "Our labor situation is better than yours, because in the United States your unions are independent. In Japan, all our unions are company unions."

For both worker and executive, the company is the center of life. Workers often display a quaint family spirit, referring to "my" company, and *my* is written with the same Japanese character that represents *family*. They often cheer each other when changing shifts, like baseball players applauding a teammate who has just hit a home run. It is rare for a major executive to leave on a business trip without getting a rousing send-off from the entire office staff at the airport. At Matsushita Electric, Nissan Motors and other firms, the day begins with everybody assembling to sing the company song. At Toyota the day opens with five minutes of supervised calisthenics. There is a vast range of fringe benefits: discount meals at plant cafeterias, cut-rate vacations at company resorts, cheap rental in company apartment houses (roughly $10.80 a month for a two-room flat in one Nippon Kokan building in Yokohama).

The head of a Japanese company is bowed and scraped to by gaggles of company-smocked office girls, drivers and flunkies. The company-paid geisha party for executives is still common, though some newer firms are getting away from it. Almost always, the businessman's wife must accept a new form of concubine: the company. In a recent survey, 68 percent of the Japanese managers polled said that business was more important to them than their families.

Banzai for Swapping

The executive spends much time talking with officials of other companies, because the tradition of cooperative effort has resulted in a clubby Japanese-industry organization. The prewar *zaibatsu* cartels of Mitsui, Mitsubishi and Sumitomo were broken up under the US occupation and supposedly have come together again only loosely. But presidents of the twenty-seven Mitsubishi companies meet one Friday every month; it is an open secret that they plan common strategy at "the Friday Club." The seventeen Mitsui presidents meet one Thursday every month, and the seventeen Sumitomo presidents one Monday a month. The big borrowers from the Fuji Bank have a council known as Fuyo Kai, which includes the heads of Hitachi (electrical machinery), Nissan Motors (autos) and Nippon Kokan (steel). The clubs divide up markets like so much sukiyaki. When Communist China recently decreed that it would not trade with Japanese firms that do business with South Korea or Taiwan, the clubs quickly reached an understanding: Mitsui and Mitsubishi decided to concentrate on South Korea and Taiwan, while Sumitomo took China.

Japanese shipyards can overwhelm foreign competitors partly because their engineers regularly swap technological ideas—so completely that no one remembers and no one cares which company originated a certain important welding process. Says Masashi Isano, seventy-one, chairman of Kawasaki Heavy Industries: "By closely emulating each other, our engineers constantly improve themselves and the industry as a whole. All I have to say to that is *banzai!*"

Those Helpful Bureaucrats

Nowhere in the non-Communist world do business and government coexist so closely. Prime Minister Eisaku Sato heads the Trade Conference, which sets national export goals and coordinates business efforts to achieve them. Most of the government's influence is exercised by the all-important Ministry of International Trade and Industry (MITI), which issues *gyosei shido,* or administrative guidance. For instance, MITI may "advise" a Japanese company to buy a domestic computer rather than one from IBM. A few years ago, many Japanese petrochemical concerns planned to build big plants. MITI experts advised that the foreseeable foreign and domestic demand would justify only six such plants and that construction would have to be spread over three years. The petrochemical-industry trade association quickly decided which six companies should build them—and when.

Japan's competitive strength derives from much more than the government's hothouse care. The nation is developing a new generation of inventive, competitive executives quite able to capture foreign markets on their own. Their exemplar and leader is Sony's Morita [Akio Morita, the export chief of Sony Corporation, which sells radios, tape recorders, TV sets and other products throughout the world —Ed.].

Unlike older Japanese firms, Sony sells through its own marketing network rather than through the trading companies that contact overseas buyers for most Japanese manufacturers. Its basic financing is not through bank loans but the sale of stock, 31 percent of which has been bought by foreigners. Morita, personally and through a family investment company, is the largest shareholder, with 10.3 percent worth $130 million.

Slender, white-haired Morita, now fifty, is a mixture of Japanese and Western patterns. Amid the woofers, tweeters, exponential horns and other electronic gadgetry crammed into the den of his Tokyo home stands an authentic American nickelodeon that he plays delightedly with nickels brought back from the United States. As Morita . . . [says]: "Americans like to come to Japan and take home Japanese antiques. I go to America and bring home your antiques." Morita spends about a third of his time on the road, jetting so often to the United States and Europe that he jokes, "It's

a long commute." At home or abroad, he regularly arrives
at Sony's offices by 8:30 A.M. and works for twelve hours or
more. In off hours in foreign cities, he likes to stroll about
checking on store displays of Sony and competing products
and jotting observations in a notebook. "Business is my
hobby," he says.

LOOKING BEYOND THE BOOM [3]

The contemporary image of Japan as an affluent society
has been accepted abroad and is fairly convincing even at
close range. During the last decade shabby business buildings
have been pulled down relentlessly to make way for modern
if not always attractive new structures, city streets and roads
have been widened and monumental superhighways built
to accommodate greatly increased motor traffic. Private automobiles, prohibitively expensive for working men ten years
ago, are now owned by some 17 percent of all households
and home appliances have become commonplace.

Nearly every home has a television set, and color television ownership is expected to surpass 50 percent. . . . In
1960 the simple kerosene heating stove was something of a
luxury, but now nearly three fourths of Japanese homes have
them. Other impressive figures by households (1969) are:
electric washing machines, 88 percent; electric refrigerators,
84 percent; vacuum cleaners, 62 percent; and gas water heat-
ers, 28.6 percent.

The rising middle class, approaching a surfeit of mass-
produced goods, is aiming higher and buying imported luxury merchandise. . . .

In Japan's *reijah buumu* (leisure boom), golf has become a craze among white-collar employees, and skiing
among the younger set. Schools of tea ceremony, flower arrangement, traditional dancing, cooking, sewing and English
are big business, although the favorite pastime for men is
still *pachinko* (pinball), followed by bowling and mah-jongg.

[3] From article by John Roberts, journalist. *Far Eastern Economic Review.*
71:41-4. Mr. 27, '71. Reprinted by permission.

It has been reported that the average family's "sundry" or discretionary spending has risen to almost 40 percent of total expenditures as against 34 percent for food (in 1968).

It should follow then that the Japanese are a happy people indeed. Yet despite all the superficial affluence, they are confused, discontented, and in some sectors demoralized—not by prosperity itself, which they are mature enough to absorb, but by the belated realization that economic growth and the proliferation of novelties has not fulfilled their needs and has jeopardized their society.

In assessing the consequences of Japan's economic growth —which brought the GNP to third place in world ranking and raised per capita income to more than $1,300 a year—observers must come to grips with two questions: how much richer is the average Japanese in purely material terms? And to what extent has the new affluence enhanced the quality of his life?

Japanese as Asians are well-off compared with their regional neighbors. The average Japanese as a worker is not badly-off compared with his European counterpart. But the average Japanese doesn't think of himself as an Asian, and even though he may be a proletarian in the economic sense, he has cultivated a middle-class image of himself. Thus an objectively favorable comparison with Asian workers does little to satisfy his subjective desires.

The Japanese today are anything but nationalistic in the sense of putting national power or prestige above individual happiness. Study after study has shown that personal fulfillment through learning, recreation, love, home and family life is the overwhelmingly dominant value. And material prosperity has whetted his expectation of achieving a decent, secure, middle-class milieu.

In the past few years, average income per household has risen steadily to reach $2,800, the health and welfare ministry claims. But this income is not evenly distributed, and about half of all Japanese families live on less than $2,300. Wages in small enterprises (less than thirty employees) which make up the great majority of all businesses, average about $1,600. To make ends meet, at least half of married women take employment, usually at shockingly low wages.

An average bank clerk is a white-collar aristocrat. He earns about $45 a week, or one-third as much as his American counterpart, yet his cost of living is as high if not higher than the American's in normal times. But Japan is now in the grip of an inflation that boosted the official price index by 7.8 percent in 1970. Basic expenses—especially food—have increased far more.

The price of land has increased at the appalling rate of 10 percent a year for the past fifteen years. While inflation erodes the value of savings, soaring land prices make the possibility of owning a home ever more remote. . . . Thus the proportion of Japanese owning their own homes, dropped from 56 percent in 1960 to 40 percent in 1968, according to the Asahi *Evening News*. And that is part of the reason people buy so many gadgets and gimcracks and are so liberal with their spare cash. As they lose hope of ever buying land, and as the value of their savings shrinks faster than their wages rise, they spend.

The average family lives in a run-down, drafty wooden house, too small for its needs and cluttered with old appliances, a bed and a set of Western style furniture. If luck improves, the family will move into an equally cramped suburban *danchi* (cooperative apartment), recently constructed but with the depressing appearance of a prison cell block. If it rises higher on the economic scale the family may own a "mansion," a tiny urban apartment the only advantage of which is that it is fairly new, central, and has a private bath and toilet.

The less fortunate town or city dwellers share communal toilets; less than 10 percent of homes have flush toilets, and in the cities where the percentage is higher, most are not connected with a sewer system, so a mechanized version of the old night-soil cart—the noisy "vacuum car"—is still in operation. Privacy, which Japanese value, is not to be had in most homes, where each room is occupied by two or more people.

The "grow now, plan later" policy of the business-dominated government has led to the concentration of almost half the nation's people and most of its industrial activity in the "Tokyo-Osaka Megalopolis," a narrow strip of coastal land less than five hundred miles long, with consequent congestion, pollution, blighting of the landscape, and proliferation of jerry-built houses that rapidly deteriorate into slums. As small communities are absorbed into this cancerous neoplasm, the population quickly outgrows the social facilities. The narrow roads become clogged with cars; open sewers discharge their contents haphazardly into rivers from which communities downstream take their drinking water; dwellings, shops, chicken farms, slaughterhouses and factories rise up cheek by jowl. Public parks are scarcely to be found, and the only oases in this general squalor are high-fenced golf courses which aggravate the inflation of suburban land prices.

The most ghastly miscalculation of Japanese business was to deliberately promote motorization as a stimulant to economic growth. While the Japan National Railways deteriorated (except for its highly publicized express line between Tokyo and Osaka) untold millions of dollars were spent on manufacturing passenger automobiles and constructing superhighways and other facilities—only to spawn a social evil that is now apparently incurable.

In the suffocating smog of the cities, pedestrians and cyclists mill about in intimacy with motor cars, most of which seem to be driven by a race of hyperthyroid subhumans. Japan is about the size of California, but most of the traffic is in level areas comprising less than 10 percent of the land area. Fighting for road space in this tiny country are sixteen million cars, which running bumper to bumper would encircle the earth with enough left over to reach from New York to Los Angeles. Annual traffic casualties amount to

20,000 dead and one million injured. (The official police figure for deaths is smaller, as it includes only those who die within twenty-four hours of the accident, presumably to mitigate the horror.) As an index of the moral deterioration brought on by this plague, no less than 34,000 hit-and-run accidents were reported in 1969.

That the auto menace is having a severe psychological effect on the Japanese was indicated in a poll conducted by the American International Underwriters Company in February [1971]. Fifteen hundred employees of seventy-three large companies were asked: "What do you fear most at present?" and shown a list of six items—traffic accidents, environmental hazards, nuclear war, fires, earthquake and cancer. Answers were graduated at "most," "much" or "no fear." Topping the list of "most feared" menaces were traffic accidents (52.7 percent) followed by environmental hazards (31.1 percent). Cancer was a poor third and nuclear war and earthquakes paled into insignificance. This in the land of Tokyo, Hiroshima and Nagasaki. [The first-named city was largely destroyed by an earthquake in 1923, and the latter two cities were atom-bombed in World War II.—Ed.]

Philosophical considerations aside, existence in a state of increasing squalor, insecurity and fear can hardly be called "the good life," even with car stereo and color television. In Japan such deterioration in the quality of life, presumably accepted by this docile people, seemed to be an irreversible process. Then the Japanese suddenly caught the ecology bug and began to search their souls to see whether anything remained of the old samurai spirit. Until then, they had been merely obedient pawns in the "consumer revolution." Almost overnight, the pawns became knights and bishops, and the mass-consumers turned into mass-rebels.

A startling situation developed around the television industry when consumer groups learned sets were being sold much more cheaply in the United States than in Japan. Demanding an accounting, they discovered color sets were subject to extreme markups above production cost. Exposure of the dual-pricing system by persistent probers was followed up by demands for reduction of the "administered" prices set by collusion among manufacturers. This campaign, backed up by an effective boycott of Matsushita (the largest maker) created such a fracas that the Ministry of International Trade and Industry felt compelled to intervene, ordering the firm to reduce its prices. Subsequently, the large makers cut prices by 10-20 percent, but some dealers are marking them down as much as thirty percent and a cooperative is offering its own model at 40 percent off the standard price.

This revolt, coinciding with color television dumping charges in the United States, brought on a crisis in the electronics industry, which now claims to hold inventories of 1.2 million unsold color sets. As consumer resistance stiffens, home electrical appliance-makers are said to be cutting back production 20-40 percent and laying off or transferring employees.

A steadily rising commotion over traffic hazards, environmental pollution, adulteration of food and beverages, inflation, housing shortages and high taxes—undesirable side effects of "the good life"—has popularized the consumer movement as never before. Members of these nationwide organizations, mostly housewives, number 15-20 million, and . . . membership and militancy have been on the upsurge. Thus, what people think about their own needs, and the fears and aspirations of their families, may at long last be taken into account by the planners of future economic development.

DISCONTINUITY IN JAPAN [4]

Of late, we Japanese have often heard pleasing words of praise, such as "the miracle of Japan's postwar achievements" or "Japan ranks among the economic giants of the world."

[4] From an address before the Foreign Correspondents Club of Japan, by the prime minister of Japan, Eisaku Sato. Japan. Ministry of Foreign Affairs. Public Information Bureau. *New Tasks for Japan*. The Bureau. Tokyo. '69. p9-13.

The forecast . . . that "the twenty-first century will be Japan's century" has drawn a picture of Japan's future for the Japanese people. It is an expression I have often cited in appealing to the people for a sense of national responsibility.

According to recent statistics . . . Japan's gross national product . . . ranks second in the free world, while the per capita income of $1,110 is estimated to have surpassed that of Italy.

Furthermore, with the opening of the Tomei Expressway . . . another major artery . . . has been completed for the further enhancement of Japan's economic growth. On the urban scene, there is a bewildering profusion of construction of buildings, factories and subways; the popularization of automobiles is proceeding at a rate that exceeds all predictions, while there has been a remarkable improvement in family living conditions. In addition to this material well-being, Japan has come to acquire all the characteristics of a modern society with the dissemination of higher education, increased volume of information and the urban concentration of the population. In certain fields, the terms such as *modernization* and *modernity* appear already to be outdated. We can even say, in limited areas, that Japan has already taken her first step into the so-called post-industrial society.

However, a closer look reveals that social conditions, such as acute traffic confusion and increased public hazards, are fast deteriorating, while there is a conspicuous disequilibrium in economic and social development as seen in the housing shortage which stands in direct contrast to the glamor of the consumption boom. These strains are apparent not only as physical phenomena, but seem to have reached into the very heart and mind of each and every individual. In other words, we are witnessing the phenomenon of so-called dehumanization as the price for material development and scientific and technological progress. The causes of the university dispute, which is currently the biggest social problem in this country, can be analyzed from various angles but the most important factor here is the difficulty that the individual encounters in adapting himself to this highly industrialized society.

In any age, youth has always sought to establish its identity and has challenged the established social system. In the case of Japan, the fact that she has gone through a period of upheaval resulting from war and defeat and the fact that the tempo of social change has been faster perhaps than in any other country have caused a particularly large generation gap. Brought up against such a background, the young people refuse to accept the existing ethical attitudes and values and challenge the existing order which they consider to be obstructive to the process of individual expression.

Moreover, although imbued with the desire to discover values that supersede the individual, they have, while still without any alternative program, allowed themselves to be incited by a small minority into taking the most undemocratic course of resorting to violence. This then, as I see it, is the essential nature of the current university dispute.

In short, while Japan has succeeded in achieving modernization to a remarkable degree, she is nevertheless beset with problems that cannot be reconciled to modernization either in the material or the spiritual sense. It is here that we perceive "discontinuity" in Japan.

Reference is often made to the "dual structure" of Japan. In the past, however, this has meant the existence of heavy and chemical industries side by side with such low productivity sectors as medium- and small-sized enterprises and agriculture. This has also meant that the Japanese people, with their democratic education, while utilizing the most advanced technology, have acted in a manner that is irrational by Western standards and in certain cases have retained a spiritual structure that could be called feudalistic.

The Japan of today, however, appears to be facing a problem that goes beyond this "dual structure." To be sure, a similar phenomenon is now occurring in all advanced countries in varying degrees. However, I consider that the

Western countries have the ability to deal with this phenomenon in a much more effective manner. In other words, it
would appear that in the West, human values are being
wisely preserved and strengthened, notwithstanding social
change. It is here that one can perceive the resilience of
Western culture.

In the hundred years since the Meiji Restoration, we
have learned much from the West. In certain fields, Japan
has today equaled the West and, in certain cases, even surpassed it. However, in the process of learning, we sought
only to strengthen our national wealth and military power,
before the war, and to regain our productive power, in the
postwar years, without reference to our ancient traditions
and values, in the absence of which we lacked confidence in
what we were undertaking. For this reason, today with the
great advances in industrialization and consumer living in
Japan, our approach to the phenomena arising from modernization is lacking a firm foundation. I feel we have a
great deal more to learn from the West in dealing with such
problems as these. . . .

Japan [at the end of World War II] suffered a temporary
loss of all her material and spiritual values. That she was
able to rebuild upon the ashes of war the prosperity she
enjoys today bespeaks the youthful vitality and capacity of
the Japanese people. Assuming that these assets were directed mainly toward the rebuilding of our productive capacity
until today, then I consider that, in the 1970s, these same
assets should be directed to overcoming the "discontinuity"
that I have cited.

The task of overcoming this discontinuity cannot be accomplished by policies directed only to eliminating the dis-
content of the individual and correcting social disequilibrium. Our national energies must be enhanced and channeled toward higher targets that transcend the preoccupation with economic construction at home. In a world living
under the shadow of a colossal nuclear war potential, this
is by no means an easy task. Clearly, the Japanese people

will no longer be satisfied with a negative pacifism which concerns itself only with our own national security. Nevertheless, it would be wrong to draw up national targets that are not in harmony with the ideals and aspirations of the individual living in our modern society. These targets, while taking into consideration the special nature of the new age, must satisfy the innate human desire to create something meaningful and worthwhile.

In the case of Japan, I consider that the most worthy target we can set for ourselves would be to direct the creative capacity of the Japanese people to man's welfare and particularly to the peace and stability of Asia. The greatest political task for Japan in the 1970s is to channel the energy of the Japanese people in this direction. Externally, if Japan were to become, despite her limited defense capacity, a stabilizing force in the international community through economic cooperation and the high intellectual standards and the common sense of 100 million Japanese, and if, internally, she were to become a country creative in the field of thought and culture, then and only then, could Japan be considered worthy of being called a first-class nation.

That the Japanese people are seeking a new national objective is evidenced by the rising demand from all quarters for greater initiative and originality in foreign policy. For example, Japan is endeavoring to fulfill her responsibilities as an Asian nation by responding to the emerging trend toward regional solidarity among Asian countries . . .

In considering our attitude toward national security, that is, the Japan—United States Security Treaty, or the consolidation of our self-defense capacity, as well as, on a broader level, a nuclear policy, we must not overlook both the need to overcome the problems that I have mentioned earlier, as well as the trend of the nation toward a more independent foreign policy. Fortunately, in the last two or three years, debate within the nation on the question of security has come to assume a more realistic and objective character. The government's thinking on security policy, based upon Japan's international position and her national strength, is gradually coming to be understood among the people in general.

Needless to say . . . the first issue that we have to deal with is the return of Okinawa. Some years ago I stated that without a settlement to the Okinawa problem, Japan's postwar period could not be considered closed. However, I consider the return of Okinawa not merely the end of an era known as the postwar, but a turning point that will enable the Japanese people to reaffirm their identity and to seek a proper place for Japan in the world.

III. THE JAPANESE ECONOMY

EDITOR'S INTRODUCTION

The Japanese economy is an Asian spectacular. Skipping from one soaring gross national product figure to another and moving ahead at a dizzying pace, Japan's output quadrupled during the 1960s—and may quadruple again in the 1970s. This section presents a comprehensive view of the economy, both within Japan and throughout the Asian region.

The first article shows that Japan's present economic growth and strength had its origins in the late nineteenth century and that industrial and human resources have been developed systematically for generations. The author also explores the possibility of developing countries' learning from the Japanese experience. The next article offers a view of the inner operations of the Japanese business system and tries to explain what makes the apparatus function as it does. The following selection, by a Japanese correspondent, examines the workings of the huge trusts which manage a large proportion of the Japanese economy.

The article "Japan—Salesman to the World" describes the dedication and determination with which the Japanese are moving throughout the world. In Asia, Africa, the Middle East, the Americas, and Europe the Japanese are vigorously and successfully selling their country's products and helping Japan establish a global economy. The following selection examines various aspects of the economy, particularly in terms of government efforts to aid trade expansion.

Next, a *U.S. News & World Report* article concentrates on the extraordinary performance of the automobile industry, now producing some 5.5 million vehicles a year. The Japanese have their sights set on overtaking the United States, which produces about 9 million units annually.

A selection from the *Far Eastern Economic Review* analyzes Japan's economic relations with each of the other Asian nations. From this discussion it can be seen that Japan is of major trading importance to every country of the region, both as a source of imports and as a market for exports, particularly of raw materials and primary commodities.

The next article asks whether Japan is able to "conquer" Asia and the rest of the world by economic means. Some Asian countries fear they may succumb to Japanese economic domination. However, as the author notes, this fear is exaggerated. The Japanese economy can be expected to continue its growth, but there is little indication that some of the other countries will not be able to hold their own.

The economic confrontation between Japan and the United States is taken up in a *Newsweek* article, and the final selection analyzes the implications of the recently imposed surtax.

THE PHENOMENAL ECONOMY [1]

Between 1950 and 1960, Japan's economic growth rate averaged better than 10 percent a year. From 1960 to 1970, it was a little less than 12 percent a year, causing Japan's production of goods and services to quadruple during the decade. Japan now has the third largest and by far the fastest growing developed economy in the world.

The visible contrast between Japan and its Asian neighbors makes clear the distinction between developed and developing economies. Communist China and India are in the throes of industrialization, but together with most other states in the region they remain predominantly rural. Literacy in these countries is slowly increasing, but most of the people's horizons are still bounded by their villages. Except in a few major cities, good roads are scarce and motor ve-

[1] From *Japan—the Risen Sun*, pamphlet by Martin E. Weinstein, assistant professor of political science, University of Illinois. (Headline Series No. 202) Foreign Policy Association, 345 E. 46th St. New York 10017. '70. p 16-28. Reprinted with permission from Headline Series #202. Copyright 1970 by the Foreign Policy Association, Inc.

hicles, even scarcer. Refrigerators and television sets are luxuries enjoyed by only the wealthy few. To an urbanized American or European, most of Asia is rural and poor. If not always peaceful and secure, life is relatively simple.

Japan presents a dramatic contrast. The number of Japanese engaged in the primary sector—farming, fishing and forestry—has dropped from a relatively low 37 percent in 1955, to less than 20 percent today. More than 60 percent of the people live in cities of 50,000 or more. Tokyo, with over 10 million people, is the most populous metropolis in the world. Every Japanese city is clogged with cars, trucks and buses made in Japan. The highways and superhighways which are beginning to connect the major urban centers are heavily used. Business offices and factories operate in large, modern ferroconcrete and glass buildings. Most people still live in quarters that are cramped and ill-heated by American standards. But virtually every household is equipped with a refrigerator, a washing machine and a TV—increasingly, a color TV. The trains and buses are packed with well-dressed commuters and shoppers, carrying the newspapers, journals and books that make Japan the most literate country in the world. The mass media provide a constant bombardment of advertising. In the numerous coffee shops, juke boxes play the latest rock music or Beethoven. Over this thriving, noisy, industrialized urban Japan, hangs a pall of dust, smoke and smog.

Japan's phenomenal prosperity and economic growth rate raise a number of basic questions. First, what is the explanation for Japan's economic performance? Second, what are the implications of Japan's economic record for the developing countries of non-European origin? Can Japan serve as a model for them? Third, what are the prospects for Japan's future economic growth?

Laying the Foundations

In trying to understand Japan's economic development and current growth rate, it is most important to remember when this surge began. Japan's industrialization . . . had its origins not in the twentieth century of rising expectations, but in the nineteenth century, when poverty and social injustice were commonly accepted as the human condition. Japan's population in 1870, when the Meiji leaders were coming to power, was 33 million. Although they were predominantly an agricultural, rural society, the Japanese even then had a literacy rate of about 30 per cent, much higher than most of Asia, Africa or Latin America today. Moreover, the people had been indoctrinated for centuries in the virtues of diligence, thrift and loyal obedience to feudal lords and village heads. The ruling, quasi-military class, or *samurai*, had a strong tradition of honesty, selfless devotion to duty and a healthy respect for individual merit. In the 1870s and 1880s, the Meiji leaders themselves were mostly young, lower-ranking samurai, whose intelligence, energy and courage brought them to the fore when Japan was threatened by Western encroachment. Moreover, the values of Japanese society were secular—here and now—rather than otherworldly. They were relatively well prepared to industrialize. Economic historians have noted that many elements of the Protestant ethic, which, some historians believe motivated Europe's industrialization, were present in mid-nineteenth century Japan.

The Meiji leaders employed these human resources with great skill and patience. They planned and worked at industrialization for the entire forty years of their political supremacy—from the 1870s to World War I. They introduced Western education and technology in a highly pragmatic and selective way, aiming at steady growth and minimal social dislocation, rather than spectacular economic leaps. They encouraged entrepreneurs and capitalists, but they did not idealize laissez-faire capitalism as a doctrine. On the contrary, the Meiji government practiced close bureaucratic supervision and regulation of banking and industry, as the Japanese government still does today. Thrift, low wages and careful management assured a substantial rate of saving, which permitted capital formation based on Japanese rather than foreign investment.

When the Meiji leaders left the scene, the foundations of Japan's industrialization were well laid. Despite cyclical fluctuations, production of goods and services tripled between 1885 and 1935. Railroad building facilitated the growth of a national market. Cotton and steel mills sprang up. Agriculture benefited from chemical fertilizers. The growing population began a steady exodus to the cities, to satisfy the growing demand for factory workers. For five decades, the gross national product (GNP) grew at an average annual rate of 3 percent. The population increased from 33 million to 75 million. Per capita income went up by 2 percent a year. By 1935, industrial products accounted for approximately 70 percent of the GNP.

In short, Japan's economic performance since the early 1950s is not a sudden flash. It is, instead, an accelerated continuation of a process begun a century ago.

Implications for Developing Countries

Seen in this perspective, the pattern of Japan's industrialization and economic development has only limited applicability to developing countries today. Most developing nations are already under greater population pressures than Japan was, and most developing peoples have come to expect increased personal income, economic security and social justice along with steady economic growth—things the Japanese hardly dreamed of. In addition, it appears that most of the developing nations have neither the high literacy rate nor the degree of social cohesion and discipline which Japan had in the mid-nineteenth century. Obviously, this combination of great expectations and limited human and social resources places the leaders of the new states in a tight spot. And, in addition to their economic problems, many of the new governing elites are troubled by much more serious and deeper ideological cleavages than those that beset the Meiji leaders.

On the other hand, the Japanese model does hold several useful lessons and even a ray or two of hope. The Japanese experience indicated that in the early stages of industrialization, "development decades" and "great leaps" are unrealistic. It shows that the failure of most developing nations to make spectacular gains over the last twenty years was to be expected, that it should not be a reason for despair, and that the transformation from an agricultural to an industrial economy, if it is to be successful at all, is likely to be the product of 50 to 70 years of careful planning, hard work and patience.

The Postwar Miracle

A strong foundation alone, however, cannot explain Japan's pace of development since World War II. Why is it, for instance, that Japan's annual growth rate between 1950 and 1960 was considerably higher than that of the United States, the Soviet Union or the Western European states, with the exception of West Germany? The West German exception suggests part of the answer.

As the losers of World War II, both the Germans and the Japanese suffered great destruction of their factories, transportation systems and international trade arrangements. In 1950, the GNP of these states was only a fraction of what it had been in 1940. Economically the Germans and the Japanese began the decade with an abnormally low base line from which to measure their economic growth. In the 1950s Japan was rebuilding what had been destroyed in the war. And again, Japan like West Germany was rich in the most crucial resource—disciplined, skilled, energetic people. In the early 1950s, American economic aid and offshore procurement for the Korean war made vital contributions to Japanese growth. Later in the decade, free-world resources and export markets provided necessary raw materials and outlets for Japanese trade.

In brief, for Japan and West Germany the 1950s were not an economic miracle, but primarily a decade of recovery.

Moreover, recovery is not as simple a notion as one might guess. By 1955 Japan had reached its 1940 GNP, but this did not represent complete recovery. For the 1940 economy, as we have seen, was an expanding, dynamic one. If it had not been for the war destruction, the economy would have continued to grow. Thus, more realistically, recovery can be said to be complete when Japan's GNP reached the level it would have reached if the 1940 economy had kept growing. What this level would be, of course, depends entirely on the projected rate of growth assigned to Japan after 1940. This projected rate of growth rests on so many intangibles that even the most knowledgeable economists can only speculate on what it would have been. In general, however, most economists agree that for Japan, recovery in this sense was not achieved until the early 1960s and that to some extent it might still be going on.

The 1960s

If the 1950-60 growth rate can be understood largely as a result of recovery, American aid, Korean war purchases and the growing availability of foreign resources and markets, what about the phenomenal annual growth rate between 1960 and 1970? How is it that Japan almost quadrupled its GNP in the last ten years, a feat no other developed economy has approached? As we have noted, Japan has continued to be the first in shipbuilding, consolidating itself as the leader in supertanker construction. It has moved rapidly forward to become second in motor vehicle production and computers. This year, Japan's auto makers, led by Toyota and Nissan (manufacturers of Datsuns) —now well-known names in this country—will turn out 5.5 million vehicles, 20 percent of total world production. [See "Japan: Now No. 2 in Autos, Trucks and Going for No. 1." in this section, below.—Ed.] During the last ten years Japan also moved past the Western European states, including West Germany, to become third in steel production. Today, American manufacturers import high quality steel from Japan.

To understand this economic record, we should first note that the rate of personal savings and investment in Japan during the past ten years has been higher than in any other industrialized country, accounting for an extraordinary 34 percent of gross capital formation. This means that while wages and consumption have kept pace with productivity, the increasingly affluent Japanese have kept saving and investing at approximately the same rate as they did in the 1920s or the 1950s. In short, the Japanese people, as well as corporations and government, have been plowing their earnings back into growth.

A second major factor has been the effectiveness of government planning and regulation for economic growth. As noted, throughout the past century the government has regulated and encouraged business and industrial development. In the aftermath of World War II, the government's concern with economic growth became a preoccupation. During the 1950s, the Finance Ministry, the Ministry of International Trade and Industry and the Economic Planning Agency recruited the brightest and most promising of the university graduates and put them to work running the economy. While political leaders and bureaucrats in most other states have devoted much of their time and talents to dealing with foreign relations, military affairs and internal political problems, the Japanese have concentrated on economic growth. Throughout the 1960s, it has seemed to Japan's ruling conservatives that this concentration on growth has also been paying domestic political dividends and making sense in foreign affairs.

That the Japanese have been able to devote themselves to economic affairs without being diverted by foreign and military affairs and expenditures is not simply a fortunate accident. It has been a deliberate policy, formulated by Prime Minister Yoshida and his colleagues during the occupation and pursued quietly but consistently by his conservative successors, down to the present prime minister, Eisaku Sato. The United States—Japanese security treaties of

1951 and 1960 have provided an American guarantee against external attack. Shielded by this guarantee, the Japanese government, since the end of the Korean war, has been allocating less than 1 percent of the GNP to military expenditures as opposed to an American outlay averaging 10 percent of GNP. Thus, Japanese economic growth has benefited from the American military presence in Korea, in Japan itself and in the Western Pacific.

The Future

The best-known forecast of Japan's economic future is probably that attributed, somewhat unfairly, to Herman Kahn, director of the Hudson Institute. Mr. Kahn's predictions have actually been greatly qualified. In its widely publicized form, however, the Kahn forecast is a flat assertion that by the end of this century, Japan will be the greatest economic power in the world, first in GNP and first in per capita income. This forecast is based on a simple projection of Japan's growth rate for the past twenty years. In a nutshell, if the Japanese economy expands at approximately 10 percent per year, and the United States and Soviet economies continue to grow at less than 5 percent per year, before the year 2000 Japan will be outproducing both the present superpowers.

Is it likely, however, that the Japanese economy will continue to expand at its current rate? One way of approaching this question is to consider the obstacles inherent in the present economy which are likely to inhibit growth during the coming decade. Developments in world trade and investment will also be a vital factor shaping Japan's economic future, but in this analysis we will focus on factors present in Japan itself, over which the Japanese can exercise greater control.

Labor Shortage

Throughout this century, the Japanese have complained of overcrowding on their small, mountainous islands, which have a total land area comparable to California, Only 17 percent of which is arable. . . . The population expanded from 33 million in 1870 to over 75 million by 1940. Since then, the population has increased to over 100 million. The bulk of the postwar increase was generated in the baby boom of 1947-49, when population growth reached a high 3 percent annual rate. During the past three years the 1947-49 babies have been joining the work force and the consuming public. Their entrance into the expanding economy has been an important factor contributing to the recent jump in GNP. Ultimately, total production is a function of the size of the labor force and the productivity of labor. In postwar Japan, population increases have swelled the labor force, and technology has increased unit productivity.

Since the early 1950s, however, the Japanese have been practicing birth control, including legalized abortions, in an effort to stabilize population growth. At present the population growth rate is down to less than 1 percent. In terms of individual well-being, social organization and stability, this low rate is most favorable. It should be recognized, however, that the expansion of the economy has been generated partly by the rapid growth in the labor force. This growth has now passed its peak, and Japanese economic planners expect an intensifying labor shortage during the 1970s.

Theoretically, in an era of increasing automation—and the Japanese are automating—the demand for labor should drop. In practice, however, throughout the 1960s, despite the maturing of the 1947-49 babies and the exodus of labor from the countryside, the demand for industrial labor in Japan has outstripped the supply. At present, in certain job categories, there are about five job openings available for every new entrant to the labor market. In the early 1960s, companies competed on the campuses for qualified junior executives. Today, high school students are being recruited for jobs a year in advance of their graduation. Employers call this practice *aota-gai*—buying rice when it is still green in the paddy field.

As a consequence of lower birthrates, the slowing of the exodus from the countryside and the trend toward advanced education, the availability of labor in the 1970s will decrease. At the same time, employers expect the demand for labor to increase. The predictable results of this intense shortage of labor, which are already becoming evident, are increased wages and labor costs, which are beginning to outpace labor productivity. This will encourage an inflationary wage-price spiral and, depending on the rate of inflation in other countries, could hurt Japan's competitive position in world export markets.

Infrastructural and Environmental Obstacles

A second and perhaps even more fundamental obstacle to a continuation of rapid economic growth arises from deficiencies in the economic infrastructure. The Japanese, even more than Americans or Western Europeans, have concentrated on immediate increases in production of goods and services for the private sector at the expense of the public sector. As a result, Japanese cities are suffering even greater urban blight than ours. Overcrowding, inadequate transportation, and air, water and noise pollution are more serious than in this country. Japanese schools are old, rickety and too few in number. Color television can be purchased on the spot with easy credit terms, while an applicant for a telephone faces a one-year delay before installation.

These infrastructural and environmental obstacles create economic bottlenecks and generate public dissatisfaction. For both political and economic reasons, Japan's leaders will probably modify their investment priorities during the coming decade. A higher proportion of resources and capital will be allocated to the public sector. Over the long run, this shift in effort will improve Japan's economic prospects and enhance the quality of life. In the short run, however, improvements in the public sector will reduce GNP growth, since investment in certain types of infrastructure, such as pollution control and parks, produce nonmarketable "psychic" income which is not measured by the GNP. Informed opinion in Japan is coming to believe that a livable environment is more important than a rapidly growing GNP.

Social Values and the Youth Question

There is also evidence that the phenomenal postwar economic growth is itself affecting Japanese values. In particular, the devotion to work and the extremely high rate of savings and investment, which have made this growth possible, are likely casualties of the leisure and consumption boom now taking place. The Japanese are becoming credit-card bearers and installment buyers. Leisure, vacation and travel are moving the focus of life away from the factories and offices, where economic growth is generated.

Whether and how Japanese social values will change over the next decade or two will be largely determined by the behavior of the generation of students that are now graduating from the universities and high schools and entering the managerial class and the work force. During 1968-69 most of the universities in Tokyo were completely or partially shut down as a result of student strikes, which included the occupation of buildings and clashes with the police. The Sato government refrained from intervening on the university issue until the general public was thoroughly fed up with the striking students and their idealistic but violent leaders. Then, acting under a special law, the government cleared the campuses and reopened the universities. With the student strike at an end, the youth problems faded from Japanese TV shows and newspaper headlines. . . .

When the strike was in full swing, it was argued that Japanese youth were bitterly disillusioned with their country's political and economic systems and were more intent on radical reform than prosperity. Today, however, amid an intensifying labor shortage and continued economic growth, there is little evidence that young Japanese executives and workers are trying to take over the country or radically change it. It appears, rather, that Japanese youth, in company with other age groups, is slightly bored with its stability and affluence and feel that, as individuals and as a nation, they need a more significant, satisfying role. There is no doubt that this emotional, psychological dissatisfaction is an impetus to changes that will affect Japan's economic future. And unlike the labor shortage and infrastructural and environmental obstacles, the problems of changing values are not susceptible to a technical, economic solution.

The gist of this analysis is that Japan's economic feats have been essentially the result of planning, saving and hard work. Japan's unparalleled expansion in productivity since World War II can best be understood as a product of single-minded concentration on economic growth. The evidence . . . suggests that during the coming decades Japanese attention will be diverted from this fixation on the GNP to social, political and international issues. If the world economy remains sound, Japan's economy will continue to grow, but at a reduced rate. Japan is and will continue to be a great economic power. It is unlikely, however, that the Japanese GNP will equal or surpass that of the United States.

JAPAN'S REMARKABLE INDUSTRIAL MACHINE [2]

The biggest company in the world is not AT&T or General Motors, asserts a Japanese economist in Tokyo, but something he calls "Japan, Inc." Norihiku Shimizu applies that label to the whole structure of Japanese business and government—diverse and complex, but carefully disciplined and enormously productive.

"GM isn't too much different from Japan, Inc.," says Shimizu, "The government is the corporate headquarters,

[2] From article in *Business Week*. p 59-65+. Mr. 7, '70. Reprinted from the March 7, 1970 issue of *Business Week* by special permission. Copyrighted © 1970 by McGraw-Hill, Inc.

and each division of GM would be like the Mitsubishi group or the Sumitomo group. And as in GM, where Cadillac will compete against Chevrolet, the system is allowed to have some competition here, too.

"In the United States" he observes, "hostility still exists between business and government. Here, we cooperate nicely."

Just how nicely is apparent from Japan's meteoric rise to the status of the world's third-ranking industrial power, behind the United States and the Soviet Union. Its gross national product will top $200 billion this year and is expected to keep climbing around 10 percent annually. It should double, in real terms, within another seven years or so.

A decade ago, the average Japanese had a near-subsistence income, and the per capita GNP was only $460 a year. . . . The Japanese [by 1970] have already passed the British and should soon overtake the French and Germans in average income. Sometime within the next decade or two they will probably catch up with the Americans.

To complete the economic miracle, the fragile yen has suddenly become a hard currency and a candidate for revaluation. With a massive trade surplus and a robust balance of payments, the Japanese are about to step up their exports of capital as well as products—mainly for investment in Southeast Asia and developing conutries elsewhere, but also in the United States.

Long a borrower of know-how from the West, Japan is also developing more of its own technology and exporting some of it to the United States and Europe. Last December [1969], Seiko-Hattori beat a Swiss consortium in a race to market the world's first electronic watch. At the other end of the industrial spectrum, Japanese steel makers are licensing their know-how in the design and construction of giant blast furnaces to European companies.

Like all economic miracles, Japan's has been achieved mostly by hard work. But the Japanese formula for success includes a special ingredient: teamwork that embraces business and government, and workers as well. This is what Shimizu, an economist for the Boston Consulting Group in Tokyo, means by Japan, Inc., and what others call the Japanese "consensus."

Japanese companies compete fiercely for market shares, but they do cooperate with each other and with the government in ways that would make United States antitrusters bristle. Companies accept "administrative guidance" from the powerful Ministry of International Trade and Industry (MITI) on everything from mergers and the formation of cartels to imports of technology.

Commercial banks also get guidance in their operations from the Bank of Japan. In return, they borrow heavily from the central bank. Of some $63 billion in loans which Japan's major city banks have outstanding, they borrowed nearly $48 billion from the Bank of Japan, according to Toshihiko Yoshino, the bank's executive director.

"As a creditor, the Bank of Japan has much power over the big city banks," Yoshino explains. "In addition, the bank can use indirect control as moral suasion—to guide banks, for instance, not to lend too much or to increase interest rates."

The ties between business and government are tightened by such practices as "parachuting" government officials into executive positions and directorships of private companies when they retire—often around the age of fifty-five. Shuttling between business and government is not uncommon in the United States, of course, but in Japan it is part of the system.

American businessmen, nurtured on the principle of free enterprise, are often appalled when they first arrive in Japan and see the business-government conglomerate in action. American oilmen cite MITI's encouragement last year of the merger of four faltering Japanese oil companies into one strong one, Kyodo Sekiyu. The new company can expect to get preferential treatment from the government. . . .

The Zaibatsu Are Very Much Alive

The cozy relations between business and government come naturally. It is less than one hundred years since most major industries were created by the government after the restoration of the Meiji emperor, the event that launched Japan into the modern world. Then the government sold off factories, mines, and ships at bargain prices to the moneyed men of the day, and from that came the *zaibatsu*, the powerful business combines. Some of the zaibatsu were founded by former *samurai* warriors who could find no employment in Japan's modern army; other samurai became bankers.

During the American occupation, General Douglas MacArthur abolished the zaibatsu—almost. They have not sprung back fully yet, and probably never will because Japanese laws prohibit banks from becoming holding companies that could control tight business combines. But the zaibatsu are very much alive. The Big Three—Mitsui, Mitsubishi, and Sumitomo—each hold regular monthly meetings of all heads of companies in their groups.

At countless such meetings, the Japanese business "consensus" is forged—a common understanding on goals and procedures and a feeling among participants of having been consulted in the process.

Not all Japanese executives are happy with the system. Says Sumitomo Chemical Company's President Norishige Hasegawa: "I strongly dislike collective decision-making—a practice that can be blamed on the desire to shirk responsibility. We have too many committees that spend too many long hours drinking tea, with only a few people saying anything." But Hasegawa is regarded as something of a maverick among Japanese businessmen. An American explains the merits of the method: "The consensus has oiled all the gears, so that once the process gets going, it goes very smoothly. The ritual is part of this."

Foreign businessmen learn to live with the system. Says a United States oilman: "It's not as difficult in many ways to operate in this kind of economy as one might think, because there are no surprises. Everything is predictable."

Predictability breeds confidence, which is one of the major ingredients in Japan's success formula. It enables Japanese businessmen to pour larger and larger amounts into plant expansion every year. They stepped up capital outlays 32 percent last year and will boost them another 15 percent in 1970. Because they know the intentions of fellow businessmen and government policy makers, they feel confident that the markets will be there when the plants come on-stream.

Actually, Japan's imposing economic structure is built on a foundation as shaky as the quake-prone earth of Japan itself. The average Japanese company is deeply in hock to the banks, with a debt-to-equity ratio of 80 to 20—almost the reverse of many United States companies. Japanese commercial banks have 98 percent of their deposits out on loan, according to economist Shimizu.

The risks are obvious. But major companies and banks know that the government will backstop them if they get into trouble. To head off a financial panic during the recession of 1964-65, the government gave $77 million in unsecured credits to the Yamaichi Securities Company, which was in deep trouble. In another case, three competitors of Oi Securities Company chipped in $800,000 to help bail the firm out.

The ties between business and government extend to workers as well. Labor is organized mostly in docile company unions. Workers on the line and their bosses expect to spend their lives with one company. They work not just for their own advancement but for that of the company, and they take pride in its progress in a way that would seem naive to job-hopping US executives and workers steeped in the traditions of labor-management strife. . . .

American businessmen who have borne the brunt of Japanese competition also look with much alarm at the growing strength of Japanese industry. Japanese steel flooded into . . . [the United States] until the United States Government persuaded Japanese steel producers to put "voluntary" limits on their exports under the threat that Congress would impose mandatory quotas. Washington is now talking with Tokyo about restricting its exports of woolen and synthetic textiles to shield American textile and garment makers.

Japanese competition is just as tough in some other fields. Most small-screen black-and-white TV sets sold in the United States are now made in Japan or assembled in Taiwan from Japanese components. Sears, Roebuck and J. C. Penney, for example, buy sets in Japan and market them under their own labels.

"Almost no company in the States can afford *not* to buy from Japan," says an executive of a US electronics company in Tokyo.

The reason for Japan's competitive clout is not low wages any more, but a combination of factors including modern plants, rising labor productivity, and efficient management. For the big companies at least, labor is no longer cheap. Wage boosts running 15 percent annually and a growing labor shortage have led big Japanese companies to automate.

Big industry still has a relatively cheap source of indirect labor, though, in its multitude of subcontractors, the "cottage industries" of Japan. The big companies shift some of their problems to these small producers when they run into a financial squeeze. The subcontractors accept payment in 30-day notes, or even 120-day ones when times are rough. . . .

Small Business Has a Tough Time

The small companies do not get the same official protection as the big ones, and they are bearing the brunt of modernization. They are having difficulty finding workers and fourteen thousand of them went bankrupt last year.

Apart from labor costs, US companies complain that close cooperation between government and business gives Japanese companies a competitive edge in foreign markets.

Shimizu suggests that the ability of Japanese companies to operate on borrowed money is one reason for their success in foreign markets. It helps them achieve what he calls "penetration pricing." Some American businessmen agree. A US chemical executive points out that because Japanese companies have a high ratio of debt financing they can operate on lower profit margins than their US competitors, which have more shareholders to pay dividends to.

But the business issues that may cause serious friction between the United States and Japan in the next few years arise from Japanese protectionism in trade and investment. The robust state of the Japanese economy and Premier Eisaku Sato's election victory . . . [in December 1969] mean the Tokyo government has more leeway to dismantle Japan's apparatus of import quotas and curbs on foreign investment.

"The increase in our national strength will inevitably bring about the internationalization of our economy," Sato declared . . . Among other things, he said his government would ease import restrictions to hold down the rising cost of living. That would soothe resentments in the United States and in Southeast Asian countries that are increasingly bitter about their huge trade deficits with Japan. . . .

Meantime, some Japanese worry that foreign influences and the affluent life are undermining the group loyalties on which their success is built. "As a result of international exchange, Japan's traditional culture and the homogeneous nature of Japanese society are certain to crumble," predicts Jiro Ushio, president of the country's Junior Chamber of Commerce.

These influences are certainly at work today. Just how they will affect Japanese business is hard to predict. But Japan does seem certain to become an ever bigger customer —and tougher competitor—for US industry for many years to come.

Trade: Service With a Bow

No economic imperative brings out Japan's capacity for concerted effort more than its drive to win foreign markets. Just about everyone in Japan knows that the country must export to survive.

Spearheading the effort are Japan's unique trading firms, which are key components of the giant zaibatsu. In the early 1950s, Mitsui and Company, Mitsubishi Trading Company, Marubeni-Iida, and other trading companies mapped Japan's basic export strategy. Today, they still handle a big share of the nation's international commerce, though more and more individual companies like Sony and the auto makers are setting up their own organizations overseas.

Luck has had a lot to do with Japan's enormous success as an exporter. Its great industrial buildup coincided with two decades of almost uninterrupted expansion of world trade, spurred by lower trade barriers. But the trading companies turned the opportunities into an export bonanza by deciding that Japanese exporters should concentrate on durable consumer goods. . . .

Figures show how successful the consumer-goods strategy has been. Out of total exports of $16 billion last year, consumer electronic products alone accounted for some $1.5 billion. Last year [1969] Japan ran up a $3.7 billion trade surplus, $1.5 billion of it with the United States. And trade with some other nations, particularly in Asia, was even more lopsided.

In South Korea, for instance, Japan sold six times more goods than it bought. The imbalance is stirring fears that Japan may try to turn some of its customers into economic satellites. . . . Indonesian Foreign Minister Adam Malik bluntly warned Tokyo that Southeast Asians are afraid of Japanese intentions.

Part of Japan's foreign trade muscle is due to cheap, high-quality products and part to the versatile trading companies, which Mitsui's Mizukami calls "the eyes and ears" for industry back home. The companies can carry out just about any kind of overseas trade, financing, or investment for themselves, for their affiliates within the zaibatsu, or for any other Japanese concerns. Mitsui, whose sales this year will probably top $7 billion, has 9,500 employees in 100 offices around the world, including 11 in the United States. They handle everything from radios to steel on behalf of some one thousand Japanese companies.

One early signal that trading companies sent back home was the need for quality to overcome the stigma of shoddiness attached to the Made-in-Japan label. Industry was so successful in responding that a Japanese label is now a strong selling point. In Stockholm, where point-of-origin labeling is not mandatory, jewelers deliberately advertise watches as Japanese-made. In Bonn a flock of discothèques that opened last year specified Japanese hi-fi units instead of German equipment. . . .

Service to retailers and after service for customers are other important strings to the Japanese marketing bow. "American and European industrialists rely on a vertical distribution system that is built around major wholesale and retail networks," explains Mizukami. "The Japanese concentrate on servicing the little merchant. We have what a Westerner would call a horizontal marketing concept, geared to help small independent merchants. It takes a lot of effort to service these small retailers, but it is a vast market in itself."

Japanese companies apply this system around the world. In Bangkok, a small shop owner switched from stocking American electric fans because a Japanese salesman called on him, left a half dozen fans, and agreed to return in a few months to collect payment for any he had sold. The Japanese fans were popular enough, and the salesman's terms generous enough, to make him change. . . .

The next big push in Japan's overseas marketing will probably be more . . . direct investment, aimed primarily at increasing exports by shipping materials and components to plants abroad or winning markets through some combination of exports and on-site production.

Up to now, Japanese investment has been mainly in raw material sources. In the fiscal year ending March 31 [1970], overseas investment is expected to total only around $450 million. But with the yen stronger, the government is easing controls on capital outflows. MITI estimates that Japanese direct foreign investment may go as high as $1 billion in the next fiscal year, and soar to $3 billion in 1975.

Most Japanese investment will continue to go to developing countries. Toyota Motor Company, for example, has just announced plans for an engine plant in Korea, which will export 90 percent of its output. But some investment will come to the United States, Europe, and other industrial countries. . . .

Electronics: A Program for Computers

One of the major industries pushing the Japanese economy at high speed is electronics. Made-in-Japan transistorized radios have penetrated virtually every corner of the world, followed by TV and more sophisticated gadgets. Now the Japanese are reaching for an even bigger prize—they are trying to become an international power in computers.

They have a long way to go. True, Japan is already in second place to the United States in the number of computers installed worldwide. But the figures are 5,600 machines to the United States's 52,500. Again, . . . [1969's] $475 million in sales contrasts sharply to the total figures of $6 billion for the entire electronics industry. And though computer sales are expanding at a brisk 22 percent a year, this is less than expected. Noboru Yoshii, managing director of Sony Corporation, predicts that the output of the entire electronics industry will keep growing by 25 percent a year for the next five years. By 1980, he says, it will account for 10 percent of Japan's GNP.

The consumer products makers—Sony, Matsushita, Sharp, and a host of others—put Japan in the big leagues in the electronics business. They are still the fastest-moving part of the industry, and are also the star performers on the Tokyo stock exchange.

In the coming fiscal year, MITI predicts that Japan's electronics makers will catch up with the United States in color TV output, with a total of 6.5 million sets. Other production forecasts: 7 million black-and-white TVs, 6 million stereophonic components systems, 35 million transistor radios, and more than 10 million tape recorders.

The Japanese started a revolution in consumer electronics by putting transistors in practically everything. Against the day when the color TV boom tapers off, they are lining up some new products. Among them: cassette TV attachments that will play home-recorded or prerecorded programs, data printers that operate through TV receivers, and such items as electronic car transmissions, which Toyota has started installing in its Coronas.

Most of all, though, the government-business establishment is determined to create a powerful computer industry. MITI regards this as its next major project. "The success of Japanese policy in autos has created a kind of psychosis in the ministry," says one electronics executive. "They think they can do the same with any industry."

But becoming a big factor in the international computer business requires far more expensive and sophisticated sales, engineering, and service bases than TV or even autos. To build from the current base, MITI has made it plain that computers will be the last field in which import restrictions and investment barriers for foreigners will be eased. IBM, which originally set up in Japan before World War II, is the only foreign computer maker operating, and it is limited to two models. Though sales are expanding, its share of the $475 million market—20 percent last year—keeps shrinking. Remington Rand has a joint venture with Oki Electric Industry Company, which operates as a Japanese company using local components. . . .

The computer companies and government are also cooperating on software and marketing. Fujitsu, NEC [Nippon Electric Company], and Hitachi set up Nippon Software Company with a government subsidy. All six manufacturers have also joined forces to form Japan Electronic Computer Company (JECC) to finance rentals. This effort is backed by loans from the government's Japan Development Bank. . . .

Such support helps the Japanese computer industry to grow as briskly as it has. Thanks to Japan's complex language, the computer should be even more useful than it is in the West in eliminating paperwork.

If Japanese computers are to compete worldwide on a big scale, the industry may have to consolidate. But MITI is having trouble in promoting mergers—partly because executives whose company is absorbed lose face.

Still, it is likely that the Japanese will carve off a piece of the international market.

"We expect the Japanese to be a factor in the minicomputer market in the United States within a few years," says William Leitch, director of industry research for International Data Corporation, a Boston-based consulting firm specializing in computers. US companies are also expected to set up joint ventures with Japanese companies to make terminal equipment for export to the United States. Meantime, Fujitsu has sold a medium-size computer to Automation Services, Inc., a New York computer service company.

"We are getting out of the imitation pattern," says Fujitsu's Ando, who was formerly managing director in charge of marketing for IBM Japan. "We are thinking our own way and developing our own methods."

Fujitsu has devised a system of printing the complex *kanji* word symbols of Japanese, Chinese, and Korean, using a dot matrix. Some 4,800 characters are possible at the moment, and the systems can be upgraded to 7,200. "Westerners can't solve problems like this," says Ando. "And it can be very important for Oriental peoples."

Japanese computer companies are starting to set up sales
and service organizations in Korea and are eyeing Taiwan.
After a look around the Far East, a British expert predicts:
"The Asian market is soon going to be saturated by Japan."

Living With the System

Looking down on the piece of Tokyo framed by the
window in his eighth-floor office, Ernest Barr, manager of
Nichiro Heinz Company, remarked: "In the first few days
here, there were times when I wanted to jump out that
window."

Every foreign businessman in Japan knows the feeling.
He is plagued by a marketing system that even the Japanese
call archaic, and he is frustrated by a web of restrictions
woven for unwitting foreigners by the close partnership of
Japanese industry and government. He bumbles against the
language barrier and he stumbles over Japanese customs.

Even so, most US businessmen in Japan would probably
agree with John Murray, manager of the joint-venture Nihon
Dixie Company, who says: "It's tough. But it's a tremendous
market. It's the place to be."

The figures bear out Murray's contention. The number
of US businesses with bases in Japan has risen from 280 a
decade ago to 450 today. Total US business investment in
Japan has climbed from $676 million in 1965 to more than
$1 billion. That figure is slight compared with US direct
investment in other major foreign markets, but it is phenomenal considering the problems American companies have
encountered in Japan and the mistakes they have made. . . .

Painful and Expensive Lessons

Some of the problems, however, are of their own making,
US businessmen admit. "The classic case," says Britannica's
Gibney, "is the American businessman who comes over here
and says: 'We're going to give you 2 percent and we'll take
98 percent, and we'll pay you out of the profits after fifteen

years.' " William Anderson, chairman of the board of NCR
[National Cash Register], says: "Too often, in joint ventures,
the foreign company sends a man here and tells him, 'Get it
organized in a year or two.' He has this tremendous pressure
on him and he takes shortcuts. He rushes around like a bull
in a china shop and he could really jeopardize the whole
setup."

Coca-Cola, whose trademark is as familiar to Japanese
as their own ideographs, is inevitably singled out by foreign
businessmen as one US company that has cracked the system, particularly in distribution. Not so, says Hughes. "We
didn't crack it, we just created our own." Still, he notes that
most of Coca-Cola's sixteen franchised bottlers are subsidiaries of such major Japanese companies as Mitsubishi and
Mitsui. "This is very significant as far as the political mood
of our company here is concerned," Hughes adds. "We have
Japanese companies, Japanese employees, and Japanese-
bottled products."

For many foreign companies, however, the learning process has been painful—and expensive. The classic story is that
of the American company that introduced a cake mix on
the Japanese market before it learned that most Japanese
housewives did not have ovens. . . .

The outsider also has to resign himself to paying higher
salaries while often getting the tailings of the Japanese labor
market. A US embassy spokesman says: "When a young
Japanese gets out of a university, he first seeks employment
with the government. Then, he looks to a major company.
If he can't get in a big company, he looks for a medium-sized
one. And his fourth choice is between a small Japanese firm
and a foreign company."

What bothers Albert Dresser, chairman of Max Factor
and Company, are the costly promotion gimmicks used by
Shiseido Company, Japan's major cosmetics company. "You
look at their balance sheet and you'll find they're not making
the kind of profit that American companies like to make,"
he says. "The Japanese policy, I think, is, 'Why pay tremen-

dous taxes? Why not spend the money on advertising?' So two or three times a year Shiseido invites most of its retailers to a big hot springs resort and entertains them lavishly for two or three days."

Many US businessmen say this lack of understanding by the home office is one of their major problems. International Telephone and Telegraph Corporation's Far East Vice President Howard Van Zandt says that back in the United States, "they know Japan is moving so fast, and they can't understand why we have such problems, why the land costs are so high, or why there are these building restrictions." The Japanese, he adds, face many of these same government restrictions, but accept them philosophically.

Encyclopaedia Britannica's Gibney sums it up: "You just need patience in this country. It takes a long time to establish the fact that you're here. It takes a long time to establish that you mean well. And it takes an even longer time to establish that you can be trusted."

NEW BREED OF BIG TRUST IN JAPAN [3]

Twenty-five years ago the great family-owned financial trusts of Japan, Mitsui, Mitsubishi, Sumitomo and others, lay prostrate—their coffers nearly empty, their mines and factories devastated by bombing, their few workable installations earmarked for reparations to the victorious Allies.

The huge trusts—the zaibatsu—which were accused then, along with the soldiers and politicians, of leading the nation to disaster, have made a comeback in the postwar years, paralleling the phenomenal growth of the entire Japanese economy. Now they are under close scrutiny at home and abroad as the alleged revival of militarism in Japan has become a topic of increasing interest.

Although the rebirth of the zaibatsu is often taken, . . . [in Japan] and in the West, as an indication of backsliding from postwar democracy to the prewar concentration of

[3] From article by Takashi Oka, staff correspondent. New York *Times.* p 1+. Mr. 26, '71. © 1971 by The New York Times Company. Reprinted by permission.

power and wealth in the hands of a privileged handful, there are important differences in organization, operation and outlook between the old and the new zaibatsu.

In addition, today's zaibatsu, according to the president of one company, account for not more than 10 percent of industrial output, compared with 30 percent before World War II.

Some of the changes are reflected in talks with workers and officials . . . in Osaka, Japan's second largest city, in which Sumitomo, one of the mammoth zaibatsu (sales of $2.7 billion last year), has its headquarters, and in other Sumitomo installations.

Akio Ohira, Susumu Tsuda and Katsumi Ito are, respectively, a foreman in a steel mill, an engineer in a chemical company and a salesman of steel products for a trading company, but each company's name begins with Sumitomo and is a member of the Sumitomo Group, which consists of forty-three concerns.

Before the war employees joined the holding company that ran the group, not an individual company, but each of the three men insists, with accuracy, that he is working only for the metals company or chemicals or trading. Nevertheless, each acknowledges that the name Sumitomo gives him a comfortable sense of security.

Mr. Tsuda, a graduate of the elite University of Tokyo and a rising young engineer in the ammonia division of Sumitomo Chemical on Tokyo Bay, said:

"I certainly don't feel I'm working for the Sumitomo zaibatsu. I chose Sumitomo Chemical because I am a trained engineer and I felt that this company afforded me the best chance for growth—to improve my technical talents.

"Some people choose smaller companies for the same reason," he added. "I wanted growth plus a sense of security, and here the name Sumitomo did mean something to me."

The Sumitomo foreman, Akio Ohira, who has also been a laborer in his fifteen years in the cold strip mill of Sumitomo Metals' huge Wakayama works (nine million tons of crude steel a year), drives his car to work from his own home.

"I have known the name Sumitomo since childhood," he said. "But at the end of the war the name disappeared, and when I was thinking of employment after junior high, I was told of a company called Shinfuso metal. My teacher told me that it was a Sumitomo company under a different name, so I realized it was a big enterprise, with stability and I joined."

Nails and Wire for Americans

When Mr. Ito, the salesman, went to work for Sumitomo, his job was to sell nails and wire to American customers. Now, after eleven years with Sumitomo Trading, he is an assistant section manager in the export division for steel products, and in a few years he will probably be manager of one of the company's innumerable operations overseas (he has already spent five years in New York and Chicago).

What more than security and stability does the postwar Sumitomo Group provide? And what is there to the charge, frequently pressed by Japanese and foreign commentators, that the postwar zaibatsu are simply the prewar zaibatsu revived? . . .

Discussing the changes that have come since the war, Shozo Hotta, president of the Sumitomo Bank . . . said: "The major difference between the prewar and postwar Sumitomo groups is that the holding company has disappeared. There is no control tower. There is no central personnel office. Each Sumitomo enterprise is quite independent of the other."

Sachio Shibayama, president of Sumitomo Trading, said: "We are like the British Commonwealth except that we have no queen."

Hosai Hyuga, president of Sumitomo Metals, recalled that when he went to work for the zaibatsu more than forty years ago, he signed up with the holding company. "It was the holding company that assigned you to this or that company," he recalled, "and it could shift you around from company to company too."

Now there is only the shared memory—and it is a powerful one—of men like Mr. Hyuga and Norishige Hasegawa, head of Sumitomo Chemicals, that they once worked for a single enterprise although one now heads a steelmaker and the other a chemical company.

"We hold each other's stocks," Mr. Hyuga said of the present system. "About 20 percent of my company's shares are owned by other Sumitomo companies. In some the proportion may be lower, and in others higher—up to 40 percent."

"The holding company exercised vertical control over all Sumitomo enterprises," Mr. Hasegawa said. "None of us want that any more. We want independent management.

"Of course," he added, "there are some Sumitomo companies that are weak, and which therefore depend on the Sumitomo Bank to a greater degree than others do, but we at Sumitomo Chemical, for instance, are so big that we could never depend exclusively on the Sumitomo Bank."

Like industry as a whole, the zaibatsu rebuilt by heavy borrowing, first from their own banks but also from others—wherever they could obtain funds. The banks in turn borrowed from the Bank of Japan— in other words, the state.

"Japan's economic growth since World War II is a miracle, and the banks played a primary role," Mr. Hotta said. . . . "We were not at all like banks in the ordinary capitalist world," he explained. "Before, we had to have 60 to 70 percent of our funds in reserve. But after the war we could not afford to do that. Everyone was crying for money. We had to lend out practically everything we had. We had to create credit. Otherwise we couldn't live. In the end the money came from the Bank of Japan, which managed the economy by giving lines of credit only to fields it considered important." . . .

Before the war the zaibatsu as a whole helped the country's rapid industrialization because, being large and getting favors from the government, they could take big risks. Their leaders, by and large, were nationalists and their profits were vast.

The concentration of wealth hindered the development of a sturdy independent class [of] businessmen, kept the labor movement weak and retarded the growth of democratic institutions. To that extent the zaibatsu contributed to the pressures leading to the war.

The revival of the zaibatsu, albeit in altered form, with public ownership, has taken place in a country where politics, the economy and society are far more fluid than before the war. Conservatives still rule, but there is a strong socialist-inclined opposition that controls up to a third of parliament. There is a flourishing labor movement. Paternal authority has diminished and the nuclear family—rather than the extended family, including parents and in-laws—is the norm.

Discussing the changed economy, the American economist William W. Lockwood of Princeton, a foremost authority on the subject, characterized the complicated relationships of pressure and counterpressure, of competition and cooperation, between Japanese businesses and between business and government as "a web with no spider." The reborn zaibatsu are important threads in the web, but they do not sit at its center and there is not much likelihood that they ever will since they all are more or less alike in having no single boss and developing along decentralized lines. . . .

The trading companies that are an essential element in the export operations of Sumitomo and other concerns are uniquely Japanese. Originally their function was to bring customer and manufacturer together. Since Japanese manufacturers were unfamiliar with foreign countries and many did not have English-speaking personnel, trading companies took care of all foreign business needs, importing as well as exporting. . . .

Mr. Shibayama, the head of Sumitomo Trading, who maintains that trading companies are especially suited to meet the manifold needs of the computer age, wants to take Sumitomo into such fields as urban development and exploring the riches of the seabed.

To carry out such projects will require cooperation from government. Sumitomo's relations with bureaucrats in the important economic ministries—finance, international trade and industry—are much like those of other businesses. Bureaucracy is strong in Japan, and a relatively young man who occupies a key position in a principal ministry can hold a company president at bay if he thinks that the national interest is involved.

Despite gradual liberalization of trade and capital, the government still largely controls foreign investment in Japan and Japanese investment abroad and has an important say in expansion.

Sumitomo Metals, one of six major steel producers but not among the top three, has frequently feuded with other producers and with the government over attempts to make it curtail plant expansion during recession. Sometimes the company has been forced to give way; at other times it has won concessions.

JAPAN—SALESMAN TO THE WORLD [4]

They are a new presence in the world—deferential, unobtrusive, smilingly glad to be of use. They are the transistor radio with the anonymous-sounding name, the supertanker plowing the Indian Ocean, the gaily printed bolts of cloth threading along New York's Seventh Avenue. They are regimented and camera-bedecked tourists in Paris, nursery-school cherubs in Hongkong, the members of a trade delegation smiling and tippling their way across Africa. They are the Japanese, and they seem likely to inherit the earth.

[4] From article in *Newsweek*. 75:64-8. Mr. 9, '70. Copyright Newsweek, Inc., March 9, 1970. Reprinted by permission.

Edwin Reischauer, the former US ambassador to Japan, puts it this way: "It's ironic that through our aid and through peaceful means, Japan has achieved what she couldn't through war. . . . Japan is a global economy." Even more bluntly, futurologist Herman Kahn predicts: "It would not be surprising if the twenty-first century turned out to be the Japanese century." The Japanese themselves agree, with the sure sense of manifest destiny that seems granted only to nations on their way to the top. The decade of the 1970s, Prime Minister Eisaku Sato told the Diet . . . [in February 1970], will be "an era when Japan's national power will carry unprecedented weight in world affairs." . . .

Japan, of course, has a long way to go to overtake the United States and Russia as a global superpower. But then, Japan has already come a long way, in an economic miracle whose impact has been blunted by familiarity. From the shambles of defeat in 1945, the Japanese economy boomed past France, Britain and Germany to become second in the free world last year, with a gross national product of $167 billion (the US total: $932 billion). Fueled by a startling willingness to postpone pleasure, the Japanese savings rate of 18 percent (versus 6 percent in the United States) has made possible a national growth rate averaging 16 percent over the past decade.

Lacking most of the resources for a modern economy, Japan has forged its industrial powerhouse by becoming merchant to the world—buying raw materials and selling finished goods in an endless, and profitable, turnover. These days, the Japanese are everywhere. They prowl the sun-baked sands of Arabia, selling watches to oil-rich sheiks. They sell folding skis in Austria, Toyota desert cars to Palestinian guerrillas, $30 million worth of generators in Detroit. Swashbuckling samurai have driven American Western heroes off the television screens of Hongkong. Nobody will be surprised if the Japanese manage to sell coal in Newcastle; after all, they are selling cameras and optical equipment in Germany, and they recently sold 42,000 desktop calculators to an American maker of office equipment. All told, officials in Tokyo confidently estimate that exports and imports last year totaled $31 billion, up 20 percent from 1968—and the trade balance will show a hefty $1 billion surplus for Japan. Inconspicuously, the yen has now become one of the world's strongest currencies.

All this is a bit disquieting to Japan's Western competitors. . . . Some of the resentment is directed at Japanese business tactics—not the classic outcry over cheap imitations of quality goods, but anger at Japanese bargaining tactics and restrictions that deny foreign businessmen in Japan the same advantages enjoyed by Japanese abroad. At bottom, however, the reaction reflects fear of the uses Japan might make of her new national power and prestige. It was little more than a generation ago that an armed and belligerent Japan set out to dominate a "greater East Asia coprosperity sphere," and reaped a whirlwind for the world. Will the pendulum swing back to militarism? Reischauer, for one, thinks not—but at least some degree of rearming seems inevitable. In any case, Japan's economic might ensures a diplomatic voice that will surely sound loud and clear in the years to come.

How did Japan achieve its economic miracle? A good part of the answer lies in the intricacies of the Japanese character—disciplined, group-minded and capable of extraordinary efforts in pursuit of the common good. "The company is like the father," explains a Japanese executive in London. "It looks after you for your whole life. And you give it devotion." Indeed, the Japanese see themselves not as a society of individuals, but a national family in which all the people and all the companies cooperate to make the nation stronger. The country . . . is not merely Japan—it is Japan, Inc. The very word for individualistic—*kojin-teki*—has an unpleasant connotation of pride and arrogance; and the approved emotion is displayed in the song sung every morning by the employees of Matsushita Electric in Tokyo:

> *For building a new Japan*
> *Let's put our strength and minds together,*
> *Sending our goods to the people of the world,*
> *Endlessly and continuously*
> *Like water from a fountain.*
> *Grow, industry, grow, grow!*
> *Harmony and sincerity!*
> *Matsushita Electric!*

If all this seems incredibly square or naive to the Occidental, it is even more apparent that—for Japan, at least—it works. And the cutting edges of this unique economy are the salesmen, engineers, managers and diplomats who staff the business outposts in hundreds of cities and towns around the earth. Thailand alone has a Japanese business community of 4,500. In the West, the largest is in New York, where more than 6,000 *shosha-in* (overseas trade representatives) and their dependents have set up shop.

In a nation where watching the gross national product is a gross national pastime, trade representatives come close to being culture heroes. Departing from Tokyo's Haneda Airport for their three- to six-year assignments in the field, they are usually seen off by delegations of colleagues waving banners and shouting *"banzai!"* Their exploits are publicized like battlefield heroics, and a truly dedicated *shosha-in* can get national recognition. Thus Nobumasa Kayabuki has wandered the world for twenty-four of his fifty-two years on behalf of Chuto Petroleum while his wife and family stayed home. Several of his years have been spent in remote Abu Dhabi in the Arabian Peninsula, a fly-blown oasis that paid off with a rush when it became one of the world's biggest oil producers two years ago. Kayabuki is now regarded as a "pioneer of the desert"—or, in another version, a "Marco Polo" of modern Japan.

Another hero of commerce is Shoroku Kato, a mine-company representative who found himself in Leopoldville during Katanga's secessionist war with the Congo in 1961. Kato figured that Katanga's principal backer, the giant Belgian mining firm, Union Minière, would lose some of its mineral rights in the province if Katanga lost the war. He managed to make off with a set of Union Minière maps in the middle of the fighting, stitch them into his underwear and get across the border. Kato's company, with others, is now developing a copper mine to be opened in 1972 on a site selected from the maps. "I robbed the right of Union Minière," said Kato proudly last week, "at the risk of my own life."

As Kato's caper indicates, a good Japanese trade representative is expected to go to almost any length in the performance of his duty. Indeed, critics in Southeast Asia complain that some Japanese go to even greater lengths than is normal in an admittedly corrupt region. . . . A Philippine senator discovered that one of Japan's largest trading firms, Marubeni-Iida, had quoted a price of $40 million to build a fertilizer plant, only to have the bid turned down. Later, the company bid $63.6 million to build a smaller plant and the Philippine National Bank immediately approved the deal. On its face, the proposal seemed to offer so much room for possible kickbacks that a special investigation was ordered by the Philippine senate.

If nothing else, Marubeni-Iida might be found guilty in Japanese minds of violating one of Japan's cardinal overseas policies—to remain generally as neutral, uncontroversial and invisible as possible. This is important to Japan for image mending in countries such as the Philippines, where the picture of the "ugly Japanese"—the greedy, violent conqueror—is still all too vivid. It is equally important to Japan's broader diplomatic picture. Through the entire postwar period, Japan has assumed the lowest possible profile in foreign relations. It has had almost no foreign policy except the promotion and expansion of its trade.

Following this precept, the Japanese have been as welcome with their goods in Tanzania, a black socialist country, as they have been in South Africa. In South Africa, as a matter of fact, a Japanese is accorded "honorary white" status—and therefore immunity from the strictures of apartheid—because of the importance of his trade.

In an even more adroit accommodation, five of the biggest Japanese trading companies have set up dummy companies to handle their nation's burgeoning trade with such hard-line Communist countries as China and North Korea. On trade missions to China, executives of these firms interrupt their negotiating with sessions of "self-criticism," denouncing their country's policies and their own lack of Communist virtue. Together, the five companies form a nominal pro-Peking lobby in Japan and actually support demonstrations attacking the United States, Taiwan and Prime Minister Sato himself. The arrangement has two main purposes: to save China's face in its dealing with the capitalistic enemy, and to keep Japan's trade balance healthy.

Japan's trade push has been so successful, in fact, that a suspicion has grown that the Japanese are all geniuses. Yet they have had failures and shortcomings aplenty. Seibu, one of Japan's great retailers, had to fold a blocksquare department store in Los Angeles some years back. According to trade reports, it had been losing as much as $100,000 a month. Similarly, New York importers chuckle over a recent case in which two Japanese managers, overwhelmed by the city, merely sat in a suburban apartment playing mah-jongg and writing elaborate and meaningless reports to the home office. In the end their company lost $2 million.

Considering some of the techniques of Japanese traders, many Westerners wonder how they have succeeded at all. Most puzzling is the matter of decisions. A wrong decision, per se, does damage—and costs its perpetrator a tremendous loss of "face." So the Japanese literally make group decisions. Through a long, elliptical process, all conceivable facts are marshaled, distributed, discussed and brooded upon until the decision "makes itself"—it has become the harmonious choice of everyone in the group. A Western executive working for the Japanese often sees opportunities vanish while the agonizing takes place. . . .

Japanese indirection is another source of confusion. Any clash of views is considered "unharmonious," so a Japanese goes to great lengths to avoid saying anything straight out. "To say 'no' in any situation is unthinkable," says a New York public relations executive who has long represented many large Japanese companies. "So a Japanese will make all kinds of barely favorable noises and then maybe say that he'll think about it. He has just told the American 'no,' but it is entirely possible that the American thinks he's said 'yes,' and the American later imagines he has somehow been duped."

Offsetting all these problems is the famed Japanese persistence. When their flimsy Toyotas and Datsuns bombed out of world markets in the late 1950s, for instance, Japanese auto men returned to the drawing boards and came up with the sturdy models which today have made them second only to the United States in car manufacture.

Even Japan's supposed vices may be virtues. The slow decision-making process, for instance, actually minimizes the chance of error. . . . Then too, an executive of Nomura Securities in London points out, the sharing of responsibility for a decision—by relieving any individual of blame in the event of failure—may ultimately make Japanese companies more venturesome. "We are very conservative," he adds, "but very risk-taking."

Manning the front lines of their nation's great commercial adventure, the *shosha-in* and his family lead a curiously hermetic existence in their outposts and colonies—usually gathered in comfortable clusters. They have the solace of substantial financial rewards; to assure the proper image, Japanese representatives are given handsome raises for overseas assignments.

And lavish expense accounts, *Mizu shobai* (literally, "water business"), are a way of life. After attending to business routine and ceremony during the normal business day, a Japanese is expected to go dining and drinking for the evening with his colleagues. This, in fact, is where the real business gets discussed. Normal Japanese manners are so ritualized, rigid and repressed that straight talk even between Japanese is a rarity. Without the relaxed atmosphere of a nightclub, bar or geisha house, Japanese industry would probably collapse.

All this helps build for the Japanese a formidable reputation as drinkers . . . But it doesn't help ease the loneliness of their wives, or that of the bachelor Japanese. A bachelor overseas is permitted a good deal of sexual leeway—but he may not become seriously interested in a foreign girl, on the rationale that she would never fit in back home. So if a Japanese does marry a foreigner, he is likely to find himself in the position of the young executive who married a German girl in Düsseldorf not long ago—transferred to Chicago and doomed to permanent expatriation. . . .

Whatever the individual and collective price of prosperity, there is no question that Japan, Inc., is paying dividends. For the first time in the history of the Orient, there is something approaching affluence on a large scale in Japan. The question being asked around the world is how long the miracle can keep on unfolding. Is Japan in the process of swamping all competition and creating what amounts to an economic empire?

Japan's own economists confidently predict another 12 percent spurt in real growth this year, to a gross national product of $200 billion—and they see this total quadrupling in the next decade, with Japanese exports rising from 6.1 percent of the world total in 1968 to 9.9 percent in 1980. This would be a staggering achievement, but the Japanese have created a good many believers. . . .

There is no lack of skeptics to say that such worries are grossly exaggerated. "There's this feeling that the Japanese put their shoes on two at a time," complains a State Department official, "that they somehow aren't vulnerable to the limits that other countries have." "They aren't ten feet tall," adds a Commerce Department aide.

Such skeptics can point to solid indications that Japan won't soar forever. For one thing, past growth has come largely at the expense of living standards; despite the country's third-ranking GNP, its citizens' personal income is only nineteenth in the world. They are beginning to clamor for their share of the pie and a better life, even if it means less growth. Then too, the huge investments of the past twenty years have been made with an eye to growth at the expense of almost everything else; and thus there are aching needs for spending on housing, roads, schools, sewers and the whole economic infrastructure.

Perhaps equally important in slowing the juggernaut is the stiffening resistance Japan is meeting these days from once-docile competitors. Only a few years back, a Japanese technician who shyly asked permission to inspect a foreign plant was greeted warmly and given the VIP tour; these days, he is apt to be escorted only to the plant gates. Businessmen and government officials alike complain that Japan protects her own industries too much and won't live by the rules of the international trading game. The Japanese have erected nontariff import barriers to no fewer than 109 categories of goods. While Japan argues that these advantages are more than offset by voluntary restraint in exporting other goods, resentment persists—and the United States, for one, is at an impasse in its immensely complex talks with the Japanese over a number of trade issues, notably voluntary quotas on Japanese textile exports. . . .

Whether this resentment and the needs of the domestic economy will curb Japan's expansion remains to be seen—but there is certainly no visible waning yet. In any case, the Japanese are looking ahead with aplomb. To move beyond exporting and insure a steady flow of raw materials, Japanese industry has been making its first large-scale investments in foreign plants—including such ventures as a $60 million lumber and pulp mill in Alaska, a $25 million coal reserve in the United States and thirty light manufacturing plants in Singapore alone.

In addition, as Japan's businessmen see it, there is another almost totally undeveloped market waiting for them. It is a subject that most Japanese tactfully refrain from discussing with Westerners, but it is very much on their minds —and as Toyota president Eiji Toyoda put it recently, "You should not forget that we have a Chinese market with a population of 800 million just close to our country." Thus far, trade with China has been small (some $625 million in 1969), but it is growing—and in addition, the Japanese carry on a thriving commerce with Russia, Eastern Europe, North Korea and even North Vietnam.

This talent for running with the hare while hunting with the hounds contributes to unease in the West over the biggest issue posed by Japan's expansion: what use will the Japanese make of their new power in the world?

"The Japanese are in great indecision," says Edwin Reischauer. "They have a nagging worry that they cannot be influential unless they are a militarily powerful country, and that may even mean nuclear weapons. They know if they depend on American military protection, they cannot be equal with us . . . This will be the big question for Japan in the next few years."

On balance, however, Reischauer and other observers believe that Japan's deep-seated revulsion against militarism after World War II will continue to dominate Japanese diplomatic policy. In this view, Japan might compromise by increasing its defense budget from less than 1 percent of GNP to about 2 percent. This would permit accepting the invitation, implied in President Nixon's recent [February 18, 1970] State of the World message, to take a share of the responsibility for the defense of the Pacific area.

But such a limited role would retain a thoroughly Japanese low profile. As officials in Washington and London see it, Japan's future influence will be exercised less by military might than by the strings that are attached to economic aid. Japanese aid to underdeveloped nations is already large—it totaled some $1 billion last year—and Tokyo has pledged to devote a full 1 percent of GNP to foreign aid in future years. In the past, Japan has not hesitated to make such aid completely conditional on a satisfactory level of exports to the aided nation; in fact, politicians in underdeveloped countries have complained that Japanese help is really nothing more than sales promotion.

Puzzling as it seems to Westerners, then, Japan's aim would be to use its economic power simply to do more business. And if such a national goal seems less than glorious, it would still be a good deal less disturbing to the rest of the world than an ambition to walk tall and brandish nuclear weapons. As Samuel Johnson once remarked, "There are few ways in which a man can be more innocently employed than in getting money"—and that truth surely applies to nations, too.

THE LIFELINE OF TRADE [5]

Japan's genius . . . lies in going other nations one better in the production and marketing of many standard industrial items. It is now the world's number 1 shipbuilder, number 2 automobile manufacturer, number 3 steel producer. These items, plus Japanese chemicals, cameras, heavy machinery, computers and electronic components, plywood products, precision instruments, cotton and synthetic textiles, compete successfully on world markets by combining quality with economy.

To live, Japan must trade. Although only about a tenth of its total output is exported, less than the British or Dutch proportion, it depends on its export earnings to buy the food and raw materials it needs to survive. Except for water, manpower, timber and some coal, the country is abysmally poor

[5] From "A Great Power Role for the Rich Man of Asia?" topic No. 5 of *Great Decisions 1970*. Foreign Policy Association. 345 E. 46th St. New York 10017. p 56-8. Reprinted with permission from *Great Decisions 1970* Topic #5. Copyright 1970 by the Foreign Policy Association, Inc.

in resources. No more than 16 percent of its land is cultivable. Few observers care to contemplate what might happen to Japan's hard-won political and social stability if a serious recession in world trade were to curtail its supplies of foodstuffs, oil, iron ore and the other vital imports which sustain its people and industry.

Phoenix Arisen

In the shattering defeat of 1945 Japan's trade lifeline was totally severed; its once-great merchant and fishing fleets lay at the bottom of the Pacific. ...

For the first five years of the occupation Japan was little more than a charity case, subsisting on an American dole of wheat and other necessities. Then the Korean war pumped $2 billion of American military expenditures into the country and gave the decisive push toward economic recovery.

Jealous competitors have said that Japan has a knack for making capital out of others' adversity. Certainly its nineteenth century modernization was much indebted to a silkworm blight in Europe, which created a huge Western demand for Japanese silk at the very moment a ready cash export was needed to pay for industrial imports. More recently, the Korean war proved a bonanza; the Vietnam war halted a mild recession; the closing of the Suez Canal since the June 1967 Arab-Israeli war opened an eager market for the giant Japanese oil tankers now steaming around the Cape of Good Hope.

But aside from Japan's having borne no responsibility for any of these misfortunes, it owes its galloping postwar prosperity far more to (1) a generally booming world economy, most specifically the US economy, and (2) its own enterprising, energetic people.

The Washington-Tokyo Axis

The cliché, "if the American economy sneezes Country X catches cold," is vividly true of Japan. In 1968 close to 30 percent of its total $26 billion trade was with the United States. Japan, in turn, is . . . [the United States] second biggest trading partner (after Canada), representing 10 percent of . . . [the US] total 1968 foreign commerce, and the largest single market for our commercial farm exports: wheat, tobacco, soybeans, raw cotton.

Inevitably, perhaps, so much mutual dependence generates friction. Washington blames part of the uncomfortable $1.1 billion US trade deficit with Japan in 1968 on what it considers unfair import barriers erected by Tokyo, and is no less annoyed by the latter's restrictions on foreign capital investment.

Tokyo, for its part, also charges protectionism. Last year, to forestall an official American quota barrier, it agreed to impose "voluntary" limits on exports to the United States of Japanese steel (which undersells domestic American steel by 10 to 20 percent). Japanese textiles, automobiles and finished plywood—all competitively priced—also face mounting protectionist pressure from American manufacturers.

The Japanese worry about any abrupt cooling down of the "overheated" American economy and contemplate an end to the Vietnam war with mixed feelings. Emotionally, they deplore the American involvement in Vietnam. Economically, they have reaped a modest windfall from it: American war-related spending in Japan (including consumer spending by US military personnel and civilian employees) rose to $586 million in 1968.

We Try Harder

"The great edge which the Japanese have over us," says the chairman of the Chicago-Tokyo Bank, Bert R. Prall, "is simply their willingness to work." And, while the overall worker productivity of American industry remains immensely higher than Japan's, the latter is coming up fast—an average 9 percent increase each year.

An old Japanese proverb teaches that "if he works for you, you work for him." Today's Japanese employer treats his workers with a benevolent paternalism which strikes some Americans as outmoded. An employee is expected, and expects, to make his lifetime career with one firm. He is carefully screened before hiring, intensively trained and then entitled to a vast array of fringe benefits (from company housing to entertainment allowances) which, together with merit raises and promotions, secure his loyalty to his business family.

There is also a quasi-paternal relationship between the Japanese government and big business. The former awards special depreciation allowances to firms with exceptional export records. Retiring bureaucrats are recruited for management jobs in industry. The Bank of Japan guides the commercial banks in their loans to private business. This gives the government important leverage since in Japan, unlike the United States, many large corporations have low capital reserves and must rely on short-term bank borrowing to finance expansion. (Cash loans are still more popular than new stock issues because the average Japanese usually prefers to put his extra yen into a savings bank instead of company shares.)

The government also looks after the welfare of thousands of small- and medium-sized businesses by protecting them, through legislation, against imports and foreign capital investment. Japan's industrial structure is uneven: thousands of small, inefficient cottage industries operate alongside the ultraefficient corporate giants. About 1,300 large companies employ nearly a fifth of the country's labor force.

And today's trend is to merge, for even greater efficiency and economies of scale. Some of the great prewar cartels known as *zaibatsu*, which were dismantled under the occupation, are now reconstituted as giant trading combines which handle overseas business for hundreds of firms of all sizes. In most industrial sectors benefiting from advanced technology and ample investment—autos, chemicals, steel, machinery, electronics—big firms are absorbing little firms and even each other: A planned merger of the Yawata and Fuji steel companies would make the new firm second in size only to US Steel.

The self-effacing, scrupulously polite Japanese do not shrink from the hard sell in marketing their products abroad. "They'll cut their price 10 to 15 percent when a 2 to 3 percent cut would have turned the trick," complains one of their American competitors in Asia. They advertise aggressively through top local agencies, offer excellent credit terms and, thanks to their mammoth shipping firms, can afford to fill small initial orders which are too costly for their rivals to accept.

Add these competitive weapons to all the others in Japan's arsenal—quality products, attractive prices, fiscal and political stability, massive private investment, a minuscule defense budget, labor-management tranquillity, business-government affinity and, above all, sheer hard work. Small wonder, perhaps, that Japan's export sales are soaring by 25 percent a year, that its foreign-exchange reserves [have] topped $3 billion. . . .

But these same weapons have begun to boomerang; in one observer's words, they have made Japan "the whipping boy of protectionist forces everywhere."

Black Ships, Blue-Eyed Presidents

The Japanese phrase *kankei nai*—"no connection"—has irritated many a Western businessman. For example, when the Dutch-based Unilever corporation takes over management of its joint venture in Japan by purchasing a bigger share of the equity, the Japanese complain of foreign encroachment. But they insist there is no foreign encroachment—"no connection"—when a Japanese auto manufacturer does exactly the same thing to his joint venture in Mexico.

Experts attribute the Japanese idea of reciprocity—rather, the lack of it—to their deep-rooted, almost pathological fear of foreign invasion and domination. The specter of Perry's menacing black ships still haunts them. Today it is embodied in the "blue-eyed" (i.e. Western) company president who controls a Japanese enterprise. They are determined that the surrender of business sovereignty to foreigners which has occurred in Canada and Western Europe will not be repeated in Japan.

So they are fighting off "the American challenge," and anyone else's, by clamping a 20 percent limit on foreign-held shares in a Japanese company; by discouraging joint ventures which are vulnerable to foreign takeover; by restricting wholly foreign-owned subsidiaries to only those sectors (steel, textiles, brewing) where Japanese firms already dominate the market.

Although the Japanese borrow heavily from abroad through their banks, they do not welcome direct capital investment in their industries by foreign firms. (In 1967 net foreign investment in their country amounted to only a third of what they themselves invested in overseas ventures, from Southeast Asia to South America, from Alaska to Ethiopia to Saudi Arabia.) They do, however, welcome technological innovation from abroad. Rather than spend huge sums on research and development, they usually prefer to acquire new techniques from others through patent and license agreements.

This need, added to the strong pressures for trade liberalization in GATT (General Agreement on Tariffs and Trade), OECD (Organization for Economic Cooperation and Development) and other bodies to which the Japanese belong, has already forced them to lower some of their quota and tariff walls against imports. They are bracing themselves for the tariff cuts set by the Kennedy Round [international negotiations concerned with the reduction of tariff barriers—Ed.], and for stiffer competition in overseas markets, with their current productivity drive and their corporate mergers.

The Japanese are by no means alone in subscribing to a double standard of doing business. But it looks to many observers as if they are beginning to realize that they cannot forever disdain foreign capital investment while devouring foreign techniques, and protect their industries at home while waving the flag of free trade abroad.

Trade Winds: Westerly

About fifteen years ago one heard frequent forecasts that Japan and the less-developed countries of Asia would become heavily interdependent in trade. There would, it was thought, be a natural and swelling exchange of Japan's heavy industrial products for the other Asians' food, minerals and light manufactures.

This has not come to pass. To be sure, the *gross* volume of Japan's trade with the Asian nations has risen substantially since the 1950s. But the *relative* volume has declined. In 1968 developing Asia, including India and mainland China, accounted for less than a quarter of Japan's worldwide commerce. The developed countries of the world, however—including the Soviet Union—accounted for well over half.

What upset the forecasts? Mainly the sluggish growth of the Asian economies, which curtails their ability to pay for Japanese imports, even though a number of them have benefited from Japanese war reparations and special export credits. There are of course exceptions: Taiwan, South Korea, Thailand and the Philippines, which have all made successful use of American economic aid and/or military expenditures, are especially good customers of Japan.

Today the trade winds blow strongest between Japan and the rich Western countries on the Pacific rim. After the United States, Australia and Canada are its chief partners. Trade with Western Europe, especially West Germany and Britain, is also growing, but less rapidly; Japan now does more business with Latin America than with the Common Market.

JAPAN: NOW NO. 2 IN AUTOS, TRUCKS
AND GOING FOR NO. 1 [6]

Reprinted from *U.S. News & World Report*.

Chalk up another field in which Japan is challenging the United States for world leadership—the production of motor vehicles.

This island nation, which ranked eighth among the world's producers of cars, trucks and buses as recently as 1955, has moved past West Germany into the number two spot and is gaining ground on the United States.

In the current year, Japan will produce an estimated 5.5 million motor vehicles. That is still much less than the US output, which . . . [exceeded] 9 million vehicles in 1970.

But the ambitious Japanese, expanding markets in every corner of the world, make it plain their goal is nothing less than overtaking the United States in its dominance of world auto-making. . . .

Mark of Success

Latest sign of Japan's rising prominence: Soviet auto officials . . . asked Toyota to help build an auto-assembly plant in Russia.

Sales of Japanese vehicles are booming in more than 150 countries. Japanese buses run on the roads of Honduras and the Congo. Trucks from Japan have become a familiar sight in Europe as well as Asia. Japanese cars have displaced US brands in the Philippines.

Nowhere is Japan trying harder to make inroads than in the United States.

Sale of Japanese cars in the United States is six times as big as four years ago, and there is no end in sight to this trend. During the first four months of 1970, Toyota and Datsun accounted for 20 percent of all imports sold in the United States.

[6] From article in *U.S. News & World Report*. 68:42-3. Je. 1, '70.

Two other Japanese companies—Honda and Toyo Kogyo —have announced plans to enter the American market in volume this summer [1970]. . . .

It is much the same story around the world. Japanese auto exports are up 500 percent in just six years. They passed the 850,000-vehicle mark in 1969, or nearly 20 percent of Japan's total output. The target is 30 percent or more, and some forecasters predict exports of 2.6 million vehicles by 1975.

Sales Aid

For all the vigor in exports, the biggest force in Japan's phenomenal boom has been unprecedented prosperity in the home market.

The automobile age has arrived in a blare of horns. Traffic is a nightmare. There are 1,200 driving schools, more than 25 million licensed drivers. Every Japanese wants to own a car, even if only one of the "midgets" with motor cycle-size engines that make up about one third of total vehicle output here.

Significantly, Japanese buyers are virtually forced to choose Japanese vehicles. No other country has so successfully blocked out the rest of the world's major auto producers. Prohibitive taxes and tariffs stifle imports. Assembly of foreign vehicles here is forbidden. Last year, import sales were a paltry 17,413 in a market of 4.5 million units.

Imports were supposedly liberalized in 1965 when tariffs were lowered on large cars. But autos of such size are not suitable in many parts of this country. A proposed relaxation of rules on foreign investment in October 1971, is considered equally inconsequential.

Restrictions Retained

Foreign investment will be permitted. However, an outsider must have a Japanese partner, can have only, at most, a 50 percent share in a firm and even then can only take part in new ventures which do not involve existing Japanese plants.

In effect, say critics, foreign firms will continue to be shut out for at least another five years.

Both General Motors and Ford assembled vehicles in Japan prior to World War II, but were forced to close in 1936 by a government unwilling to share the market with foreigners. Attitudes have not noticeably changed.

One Japanese government official explains: "We strongly fear a foreign takeover of our auto industry, since we know what the Americans did in Europe."

Behind this protectionist wall, the Japanese auto industry is thriving. It is second only to steel in annual sales and in the value of its exports.

Mergers have reduced the auto field from 11 companies to 5 in five years, giving the survivors even more muscle. Toyota and Nissan, which markets its products worldwide under the Datsun name, have gobbled up nearly 75 percent of the domestic market.

Mistakes Corrected

Abroad, the Japanese have proved to be shrewd businessmen. Like many others, they took their lumps in the US market in the early 1960s when their cars proved unsuitable to American conditions. But they learned their lessons well.

Japanese cars have been redesigned, inside and out, improving both style and durability. And when Japanese auto makers stepped up efforts in the United States, they moved with caution, taking care to establish substantial service and parts operations.

The Japanese are willing to assemble abroad, if necessary, to gain a share of a potential market. They have 60 plants in 23 countries, including one in Canada. These are wholly Japanese-owned if possible, joint ventures with local businessmen if required. All Japanese vehicles sold in the United States come from Japan.

The Japanese benefit at home from a diligent, disciplined work force. Production flows steadily. Go-slow tactics and strikes are unheard of. Auto workers are among the best paid in the country, although their take-home pay is only about one quarter of their counterparts' in Detroit.

"Selling at Loss"

Wherever the Japanese sell, their prices are invariably right for the market. A standard accusation, stoutly denied in Tokyo, is that "Japanese producers are willing to sell at a loss for ten years to establish a new market."

The charge is difficult to prove. But in one celebrated case, the Australians threatened antidumping taxes and import quotas on Japanese cars unless prices were raised $100 per unit. They were.

Detroit engineers give Datsun and Toyota good marks for quality. Says one: "These are substantial little cars and their trim often matches what we offer in our big models. I could swear it had come from our shop."

As the American companies prepare to build their own small cars, there are indications they regard the Japanese as more formidable competition than Volkswagen, by far the biggest-selling foreign auto in the United States.

US Strategy

Chevrolet has been running road tests of its Vega 2300 minicar against Ford's Maverick and the Toyota to compare performance, ride and handling. Ford executives say privately they consider Toyota and Datsun "much more like American cars than the VW is." One official adds: "We can't call the 'Beetle' a fad, because it's been around too long. But some day the string is going to run out. You can't build the same car forever. The Japanese are willing to innovate and to modernize. We've really got to watch them."

The American Big Three—General Motors, Ford and Chrysler—have stepped up their attempts to unravel the red tape that keeps them out of Japan.

Subject to Japanese government approval, Chrysler has negotiated a 35 percent interest in a joint venture with Mitsubishi Heavy Industries, Ltd., which recently spun off a separate motor-vehicle company. As explained by Chrysler, the new firm would take over all Mitsubishi vehicle production and add assembly of a Chrysler model or two. All this, however, would take considerable time to implement.

It is an open secret . . . in Tokyo that Ford is angling for a tie-up with Toyo Kogyo, the number three Japanese producer, with whom the American firm is already linked in the production of automatic transmissions.

General Motors' plans for Japan remain obscure. GM does not favor joint ventures. On occasion, it will license a foreign distributor to assemble GM cars. General Motors is negotiating such an arrangement in nearby South Korea.

Japan's attraction for US companies is as a manufacturing base, for both the Asian and US markets. Production costs are low and shipment costs across the Pacific are relatively cheap.

A Big Gamble?

The Japanese recognize the risk of US retaliation as long as the American companies are effectively barred. But strategists here are gambling that they can get away with their double standard in automotive marketing for several more years—and minimize the impact of foreign competition in Japan indefinitely.

There is no particular fear that the new American mini-cars will crimp the US market for Japanese vehicles. The conclusion in Tokyo is that standard-sized US models, not foreign cars, will be the chief sales losers.

At least one government planner . . . [in Tokyo] foresees a day when Japan may supply half of the world's motor vehicles, as it does now in shipbuilding. This, admittedly, is still a distant target. But there is no visible limit on Japanese ambitions or capability.

"Who knows? Maybe one of these days some Japanese company will buy up American Motors," suggests a US businessman here. "It would move Japan another leg along the way to first place in world automobile production."

JAPAN AND THE REGION [7]

It is hard today to mention the word *Australia* and *trade* without a third word, *Japan*, slipping out. This is because the economies of the two nations become more and more interlocked with each passing year. Rather like the major characters in a play both nations know their regional roles perfectly: fate has ascribed them the two dominant parts in Asia's economic future.

The trading relationship between Australia and Japan is well known. Four years ago Japan passed Britain as Australia's biggest customer. In those four years it has nearly doubled its imports from Australia. . . .

This almost uncontrolled growth in trade has resulted in an upsurge in the number of Japanese coming to Australia to buy local products. In the first nine months of 1971, for instance, thirty-four official Japanese business and economic missions will come to Australia. There will also be many other private, unrecorded missions. . . .

In six years exports of Australian iron ore to Japan have risen from $816,000 to $243 million, a figure that is itself up $88 million on the previous year. Coal exports are not far behind; they leapt by $40 million to $154 million . . . while every other mineral exported to Japan recorded substantial increases. Over the next few years minerals will continue to remain the major growth area in trade with Japan. Negotiated contracts have yet to reach their peaks and undoubtedly there will be further agreements negotiated.

In 1969-70 the Japanese bought more Australian wool than the previous year but paid less for it because of a price

---

[7] From article by Christopher Beck and others, correspondents. *Far Eastern Economic Review.* 71:51-70. Mr. 27, '71. Reprinted by permission.

slump of more than 20 percent of the commodity at auction. In the current year they will probably pay considerably less than the $254 million paid last year because the auction price of the fiber has slipped by a further 33 percent. And wheat fell by nearly $12 million from $62 million to $50 million last year. Despite the fall in export income earned by wool and wheat in 1969-70, Australia received $838 million—compared with $688 million the previous fiscal year—for unprocessed primary product and resource exports to Japan.

Healthy overall gains were also recorded in exports of processed primary products. Sugar, powdered eggs and unwrought copper all went up by more than 50 percent, but wrought aluminium recorded the biggest jump from $508,000 to $13.7 million. The total value of processed primary product exports to Japan rose by $55 million to $133 million, a record. . . .

Burma

Since Burma signed the peace treaty with Japan in 1953 and became the first Asian nation to come to terms with its World War II enemy, relations between the two countries have been cordial. Bitter memories remain of Japanese excesses during the war, such as those committed on the notorious death railway in southern Burma, but these have not interfered with the development of good Burma-Japan relations since Burma's attitude has been to let bygones be bygones, hoping that the sad aberration of the erstwhile Japanese leadership which led to these events will not recur.

With the peace treaty was also signed a reparations agreement; Japan agreed to supply US$200 million worth of "the services of the Japanese people and the products of Japan" and also make a $50 million loan to Burma over ten years. Diplomatic relations were established following this agreement, with the leaders of both countries voicing their desire for future friendship and cooperation.

Friendship and cooperation grew between the two countries in the course of implementing the reparations agreement. The reparations were used largely for the urgently needed rehabilitation of Burma's war-damaged transport and communications setup, and also for building a modern 84,000 kilowatt hydroelectric power plant. . . . The first of its kind in Burma, this plant is now supplying cheap electricity to Rangoon [the capital] . . . and several other towns.

In 1963, Japan made a further grant of $140 million to Burma to be drawn within twelve years from 1965, and a new loan of $30 million to be utilized within six years from 1963 under a Burma-Japan economic and technical cooperation agreement. With the funds made available so far under this agreement, a fertilizer plant has been set up in central Burma with a production capacity of 55,000 tons of urea a year.

All these reparations, grants and loans could not but have a profound effect on the pattern of Burma's foreign trade. Formerly integrated with the sterling area, trade turned more towards Japan, a trend accelerated by Burma's abrogation since 1953 of the Ottawa Agreement by which preferential tariffs were accorded to countries of the British Commonwealth. The immediate result was the replacement of India by Japan as the foremost supplier of Burma. Before the war, as much as 55 percent of Burma's imports came from India, and only 8 percent from Japan. But in 1959, 20.3 percent (the highest) came from Japan, 17.8 percent from Britain and only 10.8 percent from India. Japan was still in the lead in 1968-69 . . . supplying over 22 percent of Burma's total imports.

Recent events indicate closer cooperation between the two countries is in the offing. In January . . . [1971] a team of Japanese engineers visited Rangoon to advise their Burmese counterparts on the construction of earthquake-resistant buildings in Burma. Early in February, a Japanese economic mission came for talks with Burmese authorities in the fields of planning, mining, industry, banking and trade. Later in the month came a Japanese petroleum trade mission, apparently in connection with Prime Minister Sato's pledge

. . . that Japan would extend to Burma financial and technological assistance for development of oil resources off
Burma's western coast.

Ceylon

Commodity aid totaling US$5 million granted by Japan
to Ceylon in January marks the sixth time such assistance
has been given in the past five years. The loan, for the pur-
chase of fertilizer, steel plates, tires, tubes and fishing de-
vices, is redeemable in twenty years with a grace period of
seven years.

Japan has also provided Ceylon with credits under program aid, through the provision of experts, training facilities and grants of equipment for US$20 million. . . . More
than 200 Ceylonese have received scholarships and training
facilities from the Japanese government which has also provided the services of 109 experts in various fields.

Japan has helped out in health projects too, with training
facilities, experts and equipment. Ceylon's central agricultural research institute, a fisheries training center and the
fisheries corporation of Ceylon were equipped by Japan.

Japan has boosted Ceylon's industrial development by
substantial participation in industrial projects. Twenty-one
joint ventures have been launched in recent years. These
range from the production of glassware, shirts, bulbs, textiles, batteries and green tea to the assembly of motor vehicles (cars, jeeps and scooters). Japan has often . . . [made]
successful bids when worldwide tenders have been called
for major development projects. At present it is working on
the expansion of Ceylon's telecommunication network and
a major electricity extension project. In . . . [1971] north Ceylon was provided with hydroelectricity from a power project
in the south, through Japanese transmission lines. . . .

A large imbalance exists in trade. . . . This is chiefly
because . . . [in 1970] Ceylon allowed imports on open general
licenses and Japan was able to provide a large share of commodities at cheaper rates than other countries. On the other
hand Ceylon could offer few goods wanted by Japan. . . .

Ceylon supplies only four major commodities to Japan—black tea, coir fiber, rubber and graphite. In contrast it purchases from Japan a wide range of commodities—agricultural machinery and implements, textile machinery, fishing nets, sheet window glass, iron and steel, tires and tubes, chemical fertilizers, plastics, paper, artificial fiber, synthetic fiber, cars, buses, trucks, chains, spare parts, machinery for electricity and telecommunications, cotton yarn and thread and canned fish.

Hongkong

Japan was Hongkong's leading supplier of consumer imports for the third year in a row in 1970, but ranked only fourth among countries buying Hongkong products and third among those sending tourists here. Japan managed to corner 20 percent of the colony's consumer goods imports for the third year running, and more than 50 percent of certain sectors. It accounted for 60 percent of the value of imports of audio-visual electronic items, for instance, which include radios, televisions, tape recorders, loudspeakers and amplifiers.

Japan, in fact, looks to Hongkong as its third largest export market after the United States and South Korea. . . .

The Japanese cabinet has already passed a bill revising customs regulations to allow preferential tariffs to developing nations beginning from July . . . [1971]. A further bill will be presented to the National Diet to remove or cut import tariffs on nearly nine hundred items, not including petroleum, plywood, raw silk, silk fabrics, leather cloth, rubber or plastic footwear. Hongkong's continuing worry is concerned less with these products than with textiles. . . . MITI (Ministry of International Trade and Industry) of Japan announced it would impose a quota system on eleven categories of textiles, from cotton to man-made fibers, on the basis that low-priced imports would disrupt the Japanese market. . . . Hongkong at present pays a 15 percent tariff of declared value of goods sent to Japan. If it continued to pay this, while other developing traders such as Taiwan, South Korea and Singapore paid only 7.5 percent, Hongkong would suffer a great disadvantage in competition.

The immediate result of such uncertainty has already shown in Japanese buyers' reluctance to place heavy orders with colony dealers. A sudden slowdown in orders at the beginning of the year renewed worries of Hongkong suppliers that the impressive trade buildup of recent years would level off or decline ... [in 1971].

While these problems were being considered, efforts were under way to build up Hongkong-Japan links in other ways. Hongkong's growing packaging industry, which draws a large part of its materials and designs from Japan, was helped by the advice of two experts in the field who came here last year under the auspices of the International Management Association of Japan. The Hongkong Packaging Council hoped more Japanese experts would come to conduct exhibitions on high level packaging and give technical advice and guidance to Hongkong's growing industry.

Trade delegations between Japan and Hongkong also evidenced further links. A group of ten large importers ... held a four-day exhibition here . . . [in 1970] to promote its own machine tools, building materials and chemicals and promote expanded two-way trade between the cities. Twenty Japanese garment manufacturers are due here this month to investigate entering into joint ventures with Hongkong firms. The visit follows a Japanese survey of joint venture possibilities and mutual trade expansion opportunities conducted late ... [in 1970]. Local entrepreneurs take the delegation visit to mean the survey came up with results encouraging to the Japanese, who are faced with rapidly rising labor costs in their own country.

India

India's attitude towards Japan is marked by unreserved admiration for this industrious people who have within a brief span achieved unprecedented material prosperity, coupled with some reservations about the course democracy has taken there.

In the context of China's growing military might and the continued estrangement between New Delhi and Peking, a strong Japan will certainly be an asset to the region. Once it was hoped India would set the pace for the rest of Asia for orderly economic growth without departing from democracy or resorting to regimentation of the people. And within a specified period if India could do better than China, it would set an example for the region's other developing nations. This hope has been belied, both because of economic stagnation and lack of the necessary political leadership.

With its GNP third in the world and with its advanced technology, Japan is in a far better position to help the developing Asian countries. Yet, at least in India, there is still suspicion about the impact of a coprosperity sphere. And that is why India has preferred to go full steam ahead with bilateral relations with Japan while not taking much interest in collective action in the region.

Japan's great industrial push forward, its increasing demand for raw materials and its shortage of labor have all helped India to export more and obtain a favorable balance of trade with that country. In the early sixties India had an unfavorable trade balance, but with massive contracts for the export of iron ore the situation has now been reversed.

India's share of Japan's total imports stands a little over 2 percent. As a source of imports into Japan, India's position . . . was below that of the United States, Australia, the Soviet Union, the Philippines, China and South Africa. Nevertheless India is the largest single supplier of several commodities including iron ore, manganese ore, semitanned leather, mica, cashew kernels, sandalwood and musk. The other items in which India has a substantial share in the Japanese market are pig iron and steel scrap, raw cotton, coal, tobacco leaves, crude salt, cotton mill waste, shellac, shrimps and spices.

In the past three years an effort has been made to achieve closer relations and a number of business delegations have exchanged visits. India's participation in Expo 70 and the visit of several Japanese teams to this country have helped convince the Japanese buyer that India can supply quality manufactures as well as raw materials. This, plus the fact that Japanese manufacture was becoming capital intensive, has given a fillip to export of labor-intensive items from India.

India's imports from Japan now consist mainly of iron and steel, machinery, railway vehicles, chemical fertilizers, organic chemicals, plastic materials and synthetic fiber yarns.

Visiting Indian and Japanese delegations have concluded that the economy of the two countries is not competitive, but complementary, and that large scope exists for international economic cooperation in its widest sense and for the two countries to start joint ventures.

A Japanese industrial delegation in a report to Prime Minister Sato said the delegation was impressed with the "remarkable progress" made by India's heavy chemical industry, the scope and facilities for iron manufacturing, heavy electrical equipment, vehicles, machine tools and fertilizer plants. The delegation added that they "highly evaluate India's potential and realize how difficult it would be to attain political stability and economic development in Asia without India's cooperation." The report said economic and political cooperation between India and Japan should be reexamined both at governmental and private levels "from a higher angle and with a longer perspective."

Perhaps the most significant in a series of consultations was the meeting of the joint committee to promote trade and collaboration in Kyoto in September 1970. The delegation led by the FICCI (Federation of Indian Chambers of Commerce and Industry) observed that "enduring relationship and a sustained interest can be built up only on the basis of financial participation. Such participation can meet the needs of capital equipment easily." The delegation urged that the area of participation which has been gradually extending to spheres other than simple consumer goods should soon embrace sophisticated fields. The members felt that Japanese participation in petrochemicals and electronics could be of immense value to India; India and Japan could start several joint ventures in this country to export to other countries.

Indonesia

When a Jakarta editor visiting Tokyo recently told his host that everything he wore or carried was Japanese-made —from his socks to his tiepin—he may have been joking. But the jest was close enough to the truth to inspire serious thought, for Japan's economic presence is very real in Indonesia today.

Japan bought US$172 million worth of Indonesian raw materials in 1968, a quarter of the total exports ($688 million) and almost half [its] exports to Asia ($358 million). In 1969 Japan's share rose to almost one third of Indonesia's total exports ($243.9 million of the total $742 million). For the first ten months of 1970 Indonesia's exports to Japan came to $259.6 million, nearly two fifths of its total exports ($679.2 million), and two thirds of exports to Asian countries ($442.2 million) in the same period.

Imports of Japanese goods rose from $159 million in 1968 to $226 million in 1969. Provisional figures to September . . . [1970] put imports from Japan at $183.7 million (total imports: $658.3 million). Japanese goods accounted for almost one half of Indonesia's total imports from Asian countries in 1968 ($332.9 million), almost two thirds of the 1969 figure ($399.7 million) and more than one half of the figure for the first nine months of 1970 ($323.7 million) respectively.

Japan buys most of Indonesia's oil, which this year may reach the one million barrels a day mark, and most of its lumber of which five million cubic meters are expected to be exported this year. Of the $600 million Japan has invested in Asia, more than $150 million is in forty-eight projects here. . . .

How do Indonesians react to these economic inroads? They do not like economic dominance by Japan or any other nation. But they are also aware that there is little alternative to allowing in foreign capital if the country is to develop. The Japanese challenge, however, is met by more than just suspicion. There is an element of fear, too. Will Japan be content with trade alone?

Most of today's rulers have ambivalent feelings about the Japanese. Although all still recall with bitterness the suffering and cruelties of the three-and-a-half years of Japanese military occupation during World War II, most military leaders received their training from the Japanese. Ironically, the training made it possible for Indonesians to take up arms against the defeated, but still powerful, Japanese troops in 1945. The Japanese-acquired military skills also enabled Indonesia officers like the late General Sudirman to organize the defense forces of the young republic against Dutch attacks in 1945-50, and to lay the foundation of today's national army. Though bitter, they have occasion to feel thankful for the Japanese legacy of martial skill and spirit. Among those trained by the Japanese was the brilliant army commander-in-chief, the late General Ahmad Yani; so too was General Suharto, the present president.

Thus, some factors favor an honest, long-term, mutually beneficial economic endeavor by Japan in Indonesia. But this may not be so simple. The Japanese business people, steeled in an environment of hard struggle for survival and keen to win at any cost, usually trade as they fight—fiercely and coldly. A Japanese journalist once defended this "economic animal" habit as imperative for Japan to survive. But such an attitude could lead to hardening of anti-Japanese feeling.

In this situation, Indonesians are giving the Japanese the benefit of the doubt for as long as they need their services and capital. They are, in fact, doing exactly what they did when facing the Japanese in 1942—learning from the invaders. At the moment, there is little else Indonesians can do, whether they like it or not. . . .

Malaysia

On the economic front, Japanese businessmen show considerable respect for Malaysia's stability and see the country as one of the better investment bets in Southeast Asia. But so far only . . . [a relatively modest amount—Ed.] has been put into pioneer industries in the country; Deputy Prime Minister Tun Dr Ismail said last December [1970], however, that he thought the investment rate would grow rapidly.

Japan lies fourth in the Malaysian foreign investment league but its impact is seen as significant in the modernization of Malaysian industry. Japanese loans of up to US$50 million contain a notable proportion of aid: of this sum one third is set aside by the Overseas Economic Co-operation Fund for development purposes and has a 4.5 percent interest tag; its duration—twenty years—is slightly longer than the other two thirds which has a 5.75 percent interest rate. Both loans are tied [to the purchase of Japanese goods —Ed.] and it was their inflexibility that drew . . . [Prime Minister Tunku Abdul Rahman's] fire last year—somewhat to the surprise of Japanese officials.

The long-term view of relations was put by Minister of Information Tan Sri Ghazali Shafie. . . . Although there were worries over the rise of militarism in Japan, the minister believed Japan could be included in a multinational peace-keeping force. He made the usual demand for better trade terms, but Japanese industrialists have pointed out that as far as investment is concerned they are not exploiters of the poor as they are sometimes painted. In fact, Japanese investment in this part of the world goes largely into manufacturing rather than into secondary industry. Japan can also point to Malaysia's substantial trade surplus in most years. But in 1970 this evaporated.

New Zealand

This could turn out to be breakthrough year in New Zealanders' mental attitude to Japan. There are straws in the wind. Perhaps the most obvious and revealing is the fact that at last, after twenty-eight years, New Zealanders are beginning to talk freely about a murky incident involving Japanese in their midst during the Pacific War.

On that occasion Japanese prisoners of war held at Featherston, a camp near Wellington, clashed with their guards who in under half a minute of machine-gun fire killed forty-eight and wounded seventy-four. At the time, details of the incident were damped down, and since the war there has been no serious public discussion. Only now are the facts emerging. Radio programs and magazine articles in the past month or two have "discovered" the affair of the "twenty-second burst," evoking astonishment that anything so sordid could have happened in New Zealand.

It is just as well that time is healing wounds and facts are being faced. Already Japan is New Zealand's third largest trading partner, and as time passes it becomes increasingly obvious that the nexus must be strengthened, thanks largely to fraying trade ties with a Europe-bent Britain.

Last November [1970] it was reported that over 8,000 Japanese passports for travel to New Zealand had been issued in the previous twelve months—an increase of 400 percent over the year before. Three quarters of the travelers were businessmen, but there were tourists too, taking advantage of the Tokyo-Sydney service inaugurated by JAL [Japan Air Lines] in September 1969. In the past two years Japanese concerns have concluded big deals for supplying New Zealand iron sands to be used in smelters, timber exports are continuing to rise, and Japan is New Zealand's second largest market for wool. Only sixteen years ago this country's exports to Japan were a token NZ$4 million a year; today they are over $150 million annually and still rising.

One extremely welcome sign from New Zealand's point of view is a Japanese decision to abolish the 8 percent tariff on imported sheep meats. The tariff represents about 1.5 cents per pound and its removal will assist increasingly active New Zealand marketers to build up their sales of meat in Japan. Nor have producers here missed the point that the Japanese decision came just as Britain was preparing to impose a levy on sheep meat imports.

John Marshall, minister of overseas trade, has been considering a reduction on the duty on Japanese manufactures (on cars it is currently 45 percent, but real progress is unlikely unless Japan's 35 percent duty on dairy products is cut, lowering barriers against the one New Zealand item likely to be hardest hit by British entry into the EEC [European Economic Community].

If at the popular level New Zealanders are only now coming to terms with the Japanese, the official breakthrough can probably be traced to two key moves—the first postwar visit by a Japanese prime minister in 1957, and resolution during the 1960s of a dispute over the rights of Japanese trawlers fishing in New Zealand waters. Japan's approach to the latter question surprised many New Zealanders, who expected an initial threat to take the matter to the International Court of Justice would lead to bitter argument. But the Japanese altered course and agreed to a negotiated settlement by which they were gradually phased out of the New Zealand twelve-mile limit.

Government officials in Wellington are convinced that the Japanese have got the measure of New Zealand, not only as a trading partner and source of raw materials, but also as a state which, though small, is worth having political contacts with. There are, too, certain similarities between the two nations. Both have close security ties with the United States. Both are island states heavily dependent on trade. . . .

Philippines

A number of perceptive Filipino businessmen believe Japan will eventually replace the United States as a source of investment capital and development credits as well as the Philippines' number one trading partner.

Last year [1970] Japan not only took a bigger share of Philippine exports but replaced the United States as the Philippines' biggest supplier of imported products consisting mainly of machinery, equipment and consumer goods. The United States retained its position as largest market for the Philippines by absorbing 44 percent of Philippine exports, or US$327 million worth of goods, for the first three quarters of 1970. But Japan boosted its share of Philippine exports to $298 million in the first three quarters or to 40 percent of the total export trade.

Japan was the leading supplier of the Philippines' imported requirements last year. It increased its share to 32 percent of the Philippine market from 29 percent in 1969 or from $248 million worth of goods in 1969 to $266 million in 1970. From a negative balance of $5.7 million in 1969 in its trade with Japan, the Philippines was thus able to turn the balance in its favor, by $31.5 million in the first three quarters of 1970.

Reason for the shift in the bulk of Philippine imports from the United States to Japan has been the graduated imposition of tariffs on American goods which this year and up to 1974 will be 90 percent of the full duty. After 1974 this will rise to 100 percent. This has made the position of Japan and other trading partners of the Philippines more competitive in the domestic market.

Japan has also become a larger source of tourist earnings for the Philippines. Next to the Americans, Japanese tourists now spend the most foreign exchange in the Philippines. It was in fact Expo 70 in Osaka . . . which contributed most to increasing Philippine tourist receipts because Japanese abroad and other foreign travelers would invariably stop at Manila en route to the fair or on their way home.

It is, however, as a source of development loans that Japan is increasingly relied upon by Filipino entrepreneurs thinking of expanding their operations or opening new capital-intensive enterprises. Many Filipino manufacturing enterprises, such as those turning out appliances and electronics products, and extractive industries, like mining and logging, have made use of Japanese credits or advances.

The Philippine government itself has been relying on the Japanese government or its financial agencies for long-term credit for infrastructure improvement. Some $30 million in a long-term loan, negotiated on a government-to-government level, has been secured for financing the so-called Philippine-Japan Friendship Highway traversing the country from northern Luzon to the southernmost point of Mindanao.

Last year the Philippines also approached the Japanese government for standby credits of $50 million to help ease the Philippines' payments difficulties following recurrence of a foreign exchange crisis brought about by continuing trade imbalances and payments deficits. This standby credit will be applied mainly to cover Philippine imports of capital and producer goods that cannot be met by available foreign exchange resources or immediate earnings from exports.

Filipino entrepreneurs are likewise looking increasingly toward Japan as a source of equity for some joint ventures which are capital intensive and for which indigenous funds are inadequate and dollar loans hard to come by. Loans have been secured to finance the construction of sugar mills as well as mine mills in recent years. In the case of machinery and equipment for mining, especially the opening of new copper mines, the Japanese have readily extended substantial loans to be repaid in the form of copper concentrate shipments to Japanese consumers as soon as the mines are in production. Most big mines have been financed under such arrangements.

Japanese mining organizations have also shown increasing interest in the development of some promising Philippine mining properties; at least one was reported to have entered into an operating agreement with a Filipino group on an old copper property in an established mining producing area in Mountain Province on Luzon island.

Although Japan is not buying Philippine sugar, a good deal of financing in recent years for the sugar milling industry has come from Japanese suppliers of machinery for sugar mills that are interested in increasing their sales of such equipment to the Philippines. Although eight of the fourteen new . . . [mills] established in the Philippines in recent years have been built with mainly American equipment, six others purchased their machinery from Japan. This prompted certain local Americans to question the propriety of the industry buying most of its capital goods requirements from Japan while selling all the products to the United States.

Singapore

Japanese investment in Singapore is at a surprisingly low level; at the end of last September [1970] the total commitment stood at US$16 million which put Japan sixth on the list of foreign investors. Not only is this a low rating, it is slow growing—in the twelve months to September, Japanese investment increased by only US$1 million.

Officials explain this curiosity by pointing to the fact that Singapore is "without a hinterland"—but this is not a factor that deters industrialists of other nations. Furthermore, the two largest Japanese projects—Bridgestone Tyre and Jurong Shipyard—have done pretty well without Malaysia. But there could be a more powerful reason behind the low Japanese investment profile. What is significant is that Japanese exports to Singapore are growing by leaps and bounds; in the first eleven months of 1970 they were 30 percent up on the whole of 1969 at just over S$1,300 million. It is an open secret that not much of this stuff stays in Singapore—if it did the island republic would today be sinking under a vast pile of synthetic fabrics and cotton shirts. These sales go to Indonesia and there is little or no point in setting up manufacturing facilities in Singapore when Singapore does the middleman's job so well. Furthermore, it might soon prove sound economic and political sense to establish the plants in Indonesia itself—so again why invest in Singapore?

None of this is admitted, and Singapore remains puzzled and intrigued by Japanese reticence. Its own sales to Japan totaled scarcely S$400 million last year and obviously Japanese investment could cut this growing deficit which is a major factor behind the massive deficit on merchandise trade.

Powerful Japanese trade missions regularly visit the country. . . . The president of the Tokyo Stock Exchange has headed one such mission and the head of the Industrial Bank another. . . . There are many in Japan who see Singapore aggressiveness and dynamism as proof that the city-state is becoming a mini-Japan of Southeast Asia.

South Korea

South Korea's love-hate relationship with Japan is rooted in history. Following a century of harassment Japan forcibly occupied the country until the end of World War II. Ensuing anti-Japanese sentiment delayed early conclusion of a South Korea-Japan normalization treaty.

Few South Koreans seem to regret the 1965 amity accord which normalized relations. Yet many feel increasingly unhappy with the "economic animal" policy in which South Korea attempts to benefit from the neighboring industrial giant. They recall the pre-1965 argument that "the more we do with the Japanese, the more we are apt to lose." Seoul's weak bargaining at Korea-Japan conferences to promote mutual cooperation is often described as "crushing a stone wall with eggs."

When a normalization treaty was proposed in the early 1960s, it was seen as one way to prevent Japan from developing a "two-Koreas" policy. Much recent history of the two countries' relations in fact has involved Seoul's sensitive reactions and protests against "unfriendly acts" and "breaches" of the pact in Japan's approaches to North Korea. Tokyo's policy of stamping "Democratic People's Republic of Korea" in passports of Japanese traders going to North Korea provoked a strong protest from the South Korean foreign ministry. Seoul also resents a recent agreement between Japanese and North Korean Red Cross societies on resumption of repatriation of Korean nationals in Japan. The agreement came more than three years after an accord—under which a total of 88,600 Koreans in Japan were shipped to North Korea—expired in 1967. South Koreans charge that Pyongyang uses the 60,000 Koreans in Japan as a springboard for its espionage activities against South Korea.

Since the 1965 amity accord the Japanese role in South Korea has been rapidly expanding, notably in economic and commercial areas, and the American presence is being replaced. Despite the ambiguous Nixon doctrine and Communist allegations of Korean-Japanese collusion, any immediate collaboration between the two in military activities is not in sight. Japan still ranks as South Korea's second largest trading partner after the United States, but Korean industries are buying more Japanese plants and equipment, partly because of easier access to Japanese commercial credits and the lower cost of imports from Japan.

According to government figures the trade imbalance favoring Japan is no longer so serious: 1968's imbalance ratio of 6-1 has dropped to less than 4-1. Korean proposals at every economic conference to improve the trade gap include Japanese tariff reductions for Seoul's twenty-seven export items, which include plywood, sweaters, kimono cloth, ginseng tea, wigs and silk products. Seoul is also urging Japan to broaden a fourteen-item list of electronic components on which Japan imposes tariffs on the basis of value added in bonded trade operations.

Some 40 Japanese firms, 24 of which are trading agents, operate in South Korea, comprising the country's biggest foreign tax-paying community. The Mitsubishi group recently offered to buy US$45 million worth of Korean goods ... [in 1971]—about half of it to be reexported to third countries—in a gesture to help boost exports. The Mitsui group followed suit by making a similar offer. And most Japanese firms in South Korea assert they will not comply with the "four principles" laid down by Chinese Premier Chou En-lai . . . [in 1970].

South Vietnam

This country's wartime economy has brought Japan an export windfall. So great has been the influx of Japanese goods that they have accounted for about 30 percent of South Vietnam's balance of trade deficit in recent years. Fabrics, motorbicycles, machinery and electrical appliances have been the major purchases, US$83 million worth for the first five months of 1970 alone. In contrast exports to Japan in that period were only worth $800,000. At the same time Japan is gearing up for an expected postwar development boom.

Even in the remotest country areas it is difficult to find a household without a few Japanese-made goods. Despite heavy duties and taxes imposed in October . . . [1970] which increased . . . prices of most Japanese imported goods . . . demand seems to remain constant. To the South Vietnamese importer, nothing in the world can beat Japanese goods in terms of low prices and quick delivery. To import machinery from the United States for instance, an investor must wait at least ten months between order and delivery, and in most cases pay prices as much as four times higher. Only the government's foreign exchange resources limit the Japanese imports. Foreign exchange controlled by the United States Agency for International Development can only be used to import goods from the United States and certain other countries.

As the prospects for peace become brighter, the Japanese have taken positive steps to prepare for it in the South Vietnamese postwar economy. Last October a Japanese government economic survey mission, led by Ambassador I. Abe, visited Saigon and toured several sites of potential development projects. The mission brought back a package request

from the South Vietnamese government for a credit line of
$140 million. The South Vietnamese want Japanese assis-
tance in the form of long-term loans, direct aid and joint
venture capital participation. In October 1970 an aid agreement was signed between the two countries by which Japan
will provide Yen 300 million (about $833,000) to restore
the Da Nhim hydroelectric plant 130 miles northeast of
Saigon. The plant, built with Japanese war damage funds,
has been idle since 1962 due to security risks. Once restored
to its installed capacity of 163,000 kw the plant will generate
power for the Saigon metropolis and its adjacent industrialized areas. In December 1970 another aid agreement was
signed for a $4.5 million loan from Japan to finance the
construction of a 35,000 kva power station for the city of
Saigon. The loan to be repaid in ten years at 6 percent
interest will cover the costs of equipment and technical
service.

Japanese private investors have also been quite active
recently. In . . . 1970 Yanmar, Kubota, Mitsubishi and
IHI Shibaura have established joint ventures with local
capital to set up assembly lines for diesel engines, marine
engines, power tillers and tractors in South Vietnam. Yanmar and Kubota are expected to start operation early next
year with about 6,000 units assembled per year per plant.
In January . . . [1971] National, Sony, Hitachi and Sanyo
were authorized to build assembly plants for radio and TV
sets. [In February] Toyota also received approval to assemble
utility vehicles here. In exchange for a minimum capital
participation of 10 percent for each joint venture during
the initial phase of project implementation, Japanese firms
are granted a monopoly in exports to South Vietnam of the
particular products to be assembled locally.

Japan has also kept an incisive eye on South Vietnam's
long-range economic development. In 1963 at the request of
the late Ngo Dinh Diem, the Japanese engineering firm
Nippon Koei made an in-depth study of the development
potential of the greater Cam Ranh Bay area, 250 miles north

of Saigon. It is generally believed that this area with substantial deposits of first-grade silica sand and limestone and
a natural deep sea harbor could be developed into a major
integrated industrial port complex. From 1960 to 1965 silica
sand from Cam Ranh Bay was exported to Japan at the
rate of about 100,000 metric tons a year.

Last summer [1970] a Kaidenren study mission led by
executive director Tetsuya Senga visited South Vietnam to
look into the possibility of Japanese participation in the
postwar economic development effort. Senga estimated it
would take two years to repair war damage and build up
resources, from four to six years to develop a self-supporting
economy and eight years before South Vietnam could par-
ticipate productively in the overall development of Southeast
Asia. Senga's report noted: "After World War II Japan trod
a thorny path in the pursuit of economic rehabilitation. For
this reason we believe Japan is well qualified to suggest
ways and means of achieving the industrial development of
Vietnam."

Taiwan

In an ordinary year, anguished screams are heard from
Taiwan about the imbalance of trade with Japan. The 1970
deficit was US$346.5 million (imports of $582 million and
exports of $235.5 million). Japan even dared to chop pur-
chases of sacrosanct bananas by some $21 million. Yet the
decibels of 1971 Nationalist protest are not much above a
whisper. The center of attention has become politics rather
than trade—the politics of keeping Japan on the Nationalist
side and out of the arms of that "old debil woman" [main-
land China] across the Taiwan Straits.

With at least some of the hard-headed Japanese, trade is
the handmaiden of politics. The $817.5 million volume of
Japan-Taiwan commerce for 1970 was almost the same as
that between Japan and the Chinese mainland. However,
the balance with Taiwan was far more favorable to the
Japanese. Furthermore, with Taiwan there was no further
political price to pay. Maintenance of the status quo was

all the Nationalists asked. From Taipei came scarcely a peep about the "separation of economics from politics" under which Japan sells all it can on the other side of the river.

Taiwan reserved its denunciations for Japanese "friendly companies" which have small trade with the Chinese mainland but make a lot of political noise. As long as the rest of the trade is cash on the barrelhead, the Nationalists will look the other way. Eisaku Sato has been told, though, that Japanese Export-Import Bank credits to the mainland would be considered beyond the pale.

Whether or not the Nationalists fully realize it, they have the Japanese over a political barrel. Regardless of the powerful persuasion of some Japanese to recognize Peking, and however much Prime Minister Sato would like to please most of his people most of the time, the Tokyo government wants no part of any deal which would imply Peking's right to move across ninety-odd miles of water and possess or repossess (depending on the point of view) the island of Taiwan.

Relations with the mainland and Taiwan are in separate Japanese pigeonholes and Sato will keep them that way as long as he can. Given history and possibly the Japanese sense of manifest destiny, this is not surprising. Taiwan was Japanese property from 1895 to 1945, and not as the result of a power ploy as in Korea. The island was a spoil of war. A treaty was signed and sealed and land and people were delivered.

Some of those who inhabited Taiwan in the first half of the century came to like the Japanese, or at least to accept their ways. That may be of lesser importance, however, than the fact that Japan came to have a feeling of vested interest in Taiwan. When the Japanese coyly talk of the peace treaty they signed with the "Republic of China" and the one they have not signed with Peking, there is strong indication that they like things the way they are. To put it bluntly, those who presently rule Japan have no desire to see Taiwan handed over to those who presently rule the mainland.

Japanese pussyfoot through Taiwan these days with scarcely an audible footfall. But anyone with even a tin ear to the ground can hear those little cat's feet. More Japanese than the ubiquitous Americans are coming as tourists. [In 1970] . . . visitors from Japan totaled 177,000, which was more than 43 percent of the total. Despite its vaunted attractions, Hongkong drew only 168,000 Japanese tourists in 1970.

Scratch a Chinese mainlander with business or industrial interests in Taiwan and you probably will find a complainant whose voice is raised against the Japanese carpetbaggers. These latter are back, certainly, but their carpetbags are smartly appointed luggage full of technical assistance, moderate amounts of capital, understanding of the ways of Taiwan business and a polished sophistication about where, when and how to sell the island's rising output of goods. . . .

Depth of the Japanese penetration of the Taiwan economy is hard to ascertain. The government has cited statistics and told hard-line, Japanophobe mainlanders that the Japanese are not "taking over." That is probably true. Japanese influence may run deeper than meets the eye, however, because of the close relationship with the Taiwanese, who control the lion's share of the private means of production. The fact that many Taiwanese speak, read and write the Japanese language has been helpful. . . .

Little has been said in Taipei so far about Japan's overtly acknowledged study of the "new situation" at the United Nations. . . . Probably this is because the Nationalists are confident Japan will fight as hard as the United States, and perhaps harder, against the seating of Peking at the cost of expelling Taipei. . . . The last thing the Japanese want is a Taiwan which has been ostracized and cut adrift in a part of the world where one of the predators looks east and growls, "This island is mine." ... [In October 1971 Japan cosponsored the defeated US resolution to keep Taiwan in the UN.—Ed.]

Nationalists have loyal friends among the older generation of Japanese. Among them are Sato and other leaders of the ruling Liberal Democratic Party. A number of these visit Taiwan from time to time and have no difficulty obtaining an audience with old friend President Chiang Kai-shek. . . .

Japanese elder statesmen will not have a chance to forget that President Chiang was a generous victor. Peking has made no bones about its demands for negotiation of a second peace treaty and payment of reparations which the Nationalists forswore after VJ Day 1945. Sato and his generation would view the passing of Taiwan into Communist hands with almost as much sorrow as the alienation of Okinawa. Given the realities of geopolitics and Japan's expected role in the shaping of tomorrow's Asia, Sato's successors are not likely to feel much differently. [Communist China replaced Taiwan in the UN in October 1971.—Ed.]

Thailand

The Thailand-Japan trade deficit dropped US$6 million . . . in 1970 compared to 1969, according to the calculations of Japan's MITI (Ministry of International Trade and Industry). Japanese exports to Thailand . . . were worth $449.9 million while Thai exports to Japan amounted to $189.6 million. . . . In 1969, Japanese exports to Thailand totaled $433.2 million against imports from Japan of $167.4 million. . . .

But there seemed to be a conflict between MITI's 1969 figures and those compiled by Thailand's customs department, which indicated a [much larger] deficit . . . for that year. When the issue was raised recently, the Japanese embassy in Bangkok explained that the disparity was apparently due to different price structures used by the Japanese and Thai authorities. . . .

Thailand's customs department has not yet released its 1970 Thai-Japanese trade figures, and the ministry of economic affairs must be waiting anxiously for the figures showing an improvement, since its well-publicized campaign to solve the deficit problem has thus far achieved less than satisfactory results. During the past year, increasing impatience has been shown by political opposition parties, newspapers and local trade and financial circles about the government's ways of tackling the problem. So far, the only concrete measure taken to cut down imports was an increase in taxes and import duties last July. The government's effectiveness in slowing down the flow of Japanese goods has also been questioned.

A two-year campaign to bridge the trade gap, particularly the massive deficit with Japan, has proved frustrating. . . . Despite repeated efforts, . . . [the Economic Affairs Minister] has failed to get Japan to agree to the setting up of a trade plan between the two countries to reduce the deficit on a year-to-year basis. His efforts to get Japan to cooperate in buying more Thai commodities and to increase the number of sailings of Thai vessels in the Thai-Japan freight conference have also achieved little success. His ministry, apart from becoming a target for increasing criticism, now finds itself deep in trouble with a host of other problems including the decline of domestic prices of rice and swelling glutinous rice surplus due to increasingly limited overseas outlets.

Increasing opposition to Japan's economic inroads has been detected from many quarters. At the end of 1970, some . . . university students formed an anti-Japan club with the support of a number of professors. The idea seems to have attracted the attention of a few politicians. One MP has recently disclosed he will launch a campaign to establish a club of the same sort at the national level. But despite these reactions the Japanese business community in Thailand remains largely unperturbed and continues to strengthen quietly the foundations of its economic "empire" here.

In fact, there seems little for the Japanese to worry about. Official channels vital for the expansion of foreign economic activities have shown no signs of blocking the Japanese economic advance. The only concrete measure taken by the government which could have affected the Japanese was the July 1, 1970, increase in taxes and import duties, but this has so far not stemmed the influx of Japanese imports. The automobile market is a case in point. Although local distributors of Japanese cars reported some decline in sales, they are still doing much better business than those handling European and US makes.

THE ECONOMIC INVASION MYTH [8]

Are the Japanese "economic invaders" of the rest of the world—planning to conquer by economic means what they could not take by force in the China and Pacific wars? Is it fair to pin such a pejorative label on the Japanese, for it is certainly a damaging one? Are those who argue that the ever-present smiles on the face of the ever-active Japanese traders are smiles of the conqueror completely off the mark? Are the Japanese, to take the argument further, "conspiring" to take a hold on the rest of the world in the style of the wartime slogan "Eight Corners of the World Under One Roof" (the Japanese roof) ? For "Eight Corners" should one read the eight leading trading companies of Japan—each with its spread of offices reaching to the ends of the earth?

Such emotive questions are best pursued, perhaps, after a factual review of Japan's trading record, including its successes over the last year, which have been far from small.

Try as they may, the Japanese seem these days unable to do worse than increasing their exports by 20 percent a year plus. Each year starts with dire fears that the nation's exports will "slump," and yet—year after year—"slump" levels are hardly achieved. Instead sales overseas go up by 23 percent (in 1969) and by 21 percent (in 1970) . These results have been achieved despite the fact that the home economy was booming, with real growth . . . over 10 percent a year (in real terms) and 15 percent a year (in money terms). At-

[8] From article by Henry Scott Stokes, correspondent. *Far Eastern Economic Review*. 71:49-50. Mr. 27, '71. Reprinted by permission.

tractive as the home market was—under such conditions—
Japanese exports rose by the kinds of margins which would
send a British Chancellor of the Exchequer into the very
seventh heaven; a couple of years of export growth in Britain
at Japanese-type rates of expansion would require that
[British] Prime Minister Heath be canonized.

Last year's [1970] export performance was strongest in
Western Europe and in China. The reasons are obvious
enough: these are two areas of the world the Japanese tended
to neglect during the latter part of the sixties, partly because
the American market was so good, and so much easier for
the Japanese than the European one—and partly because of
the [Chinese] Cultural Revolution. With the end of the
Cultural Revolution the Japanese were able to jump back
into China, and increase trade to an all-time high (post-
1945) —not that the Japanese are remotely satisfied with this
performance. Last year was satisfactory, but not spectacular
in Japanese eyes; it was only natural, the Japanese tend to
think, that trade with China should have gone up by nearly
50 percent.

The successes in Western Europe—to which trade also
rose by over 40 percent—were due in part to diversion of a
whole range of items which would otherwise have gone to the
United States. At the same time Japanese steelmakers have
begun to find major weak spots in Europe's supply pattern,
and, restricted by voluntary agreement in the amount they
may export to America, they have been testing the ground
in Spain, Greece and elsewhere with standard rolled products, even venturing into Germany with special steels—
causing great irritation in the German (and the British)
steel industry.

Results in Southeast Asia were far less spectacular—an
increase of 10 percent only. The reasons here are that Japan
has in the past concentrated on those parts of the world
closest to it; and it has begun to exhaust the capacity of these
neighbors for increasing purchases from Japan. Japan has
built up huge trade surpluses with South Korea, Taiwan and

Thailand, for instance [see "Japan and the Region," in this section, above—Ed.]—the imbalance is particularly obvious in the case of South Korea—and the governments of these countries have become a little more careful. Thailand, noticing what has happened to South Korea—very much an economic colony of Japan's again—has placed controls on Japanese imports, and talked critically of the Japanese "invasion." Thai youth clubs have been formed with the specific aim of repelling the Nippon invader, though they have their ludicrous side—such little clubs tend to be led by vociferous students wearing Seiko watches and Toray trousers.

Machinery and equipment remain Japan's main export items, followed by metal products (mainly steel); the former . . . item, however, includes electrical consumer goods and automobiles and the latter were, after steel, the star export performers of 1970 in Japan. After years of expanding the home market and creating an adequate basis for full-blooded export drives—during which the auto industry was thoroughly protected from outside interference by controls on direct investment and restrictions on imports—Toyota and Nissan reached a position where they could switch their energies from the home market (now a slack one) to the overseas customer.

The performance in the United States last year was sensational. In the first two months of this year [1971] Toyota increased sales from 24,072 to 40,091 units (comparing with the same two months of 1970) and Nissan increased its exports from 9,598 to 27,661. These successes were accomplished at a time when foreign car sales to the United States as a whole went up only just over 20 percent and the market leader amongst the exporters, Volkswagen, actually lost ground in terms of absolute sales; the performance of the Japanese was all the more remarkable at a time when the leading American companies, GM and Ford, have been doing their best to counter the invasion of foreign cars with their compact cars—the Vega and the Pinto, and other recent models.

Japanese Trade in 1970

(In US$ million and percentages)

	Exports		Growth Ratios
	1969	1970	
Total	16,044	19,363	21.1
Advanced nations	8,353	10,462	25.6
US	4,972	5,954	20.1
W. Europe	2,063	2,909	41.3
EEC	971	1,305	34.8
Developing nations	6,919	7,847	13.9
Southeast Asia	4,462	4,912	10.4
Near and Middle East	629	635	1.3
Communist nations	766	1,049	37.2
China	391	572	46.3
Soviet Union	269	342	27.4

	Imports		Growth Ratios
	1969	1970	
Total	15,024	18,873	25.6
Advanced nations	7,913	10,425	31.8
US	4,090	5,556	35.4
W. Europe	1,492	1,963	31.6
EEC	821	1,118	36.2
Developing nations	6,263	7,563	20.7
Southeast Asia	2,381	3,012	26.5
Near and Middle East	1,989	2,338	17.6
Communist nations	848	885	4.4
China	235	254	8.2
Soviet Union	462	479	3.8

It is not easy to weep for the American firms, however. They still have the overwhelming share of their own market; if you visit Los Angeles or New York you see only a limited number of foreign cars on the roads (by comparison with Europe) ; and it is still something of a rarity to see more than the odd Japanese car on the roads, even in the western United States. Japanese sales to America in the first two months of this year were not much more than 75,000 units, as against sales by the American manufacturers of over

1.2 million vehicles. Japan had less than 5 percent of the market, by value. Does that constitute a major threat to Detroit? Not yet.

America is Japan's biggest market, by far, accounting for more than 25 percent of exports. Yet the sales of Japanese goods to the United States are hardly large, relative to the American economy as a whole. Thus, Japan's ability to "invade" the United States in the way it has conquered South Korea is hardly to be taken seriously. Yet, there are anxious voices in Congress these days, talking of the Japanese "threat" to the US textile industry—for all the world as if Osaka planned a Pearl Harbor of the southern textile interests. So far, as was indicated by the approval of Representative Wilbur Mills of the Japanese proposals for "voluntary" controls on textile exports to America, good sense has prevailed in America—but how will American sentiment stand up to more prolonged battering at the hands of the Japanese.

This, at least, is the impression of British business leaders. . . . [Early in 1971] a mission from the CBI (Confederation of British Industry), visiting the United States for talks with their counterparts, were told that it was because of the Japanese that there was a danger of protectionism winning out in the United States to the detriment of world trade in general, and Japan and the UK in particular. The American business world may be exaggerating on this point, may indeed be generalizing about the Japanese in this way because of the problems the Americans are having at home (on the thesis if you have a problem at home you cannot handle, blame your neighbor). Yet, sober-minded members of the CBI got the idea that it is American resentment over Japan's failure to liberalize which is at the root of the trouble.

Of course, it's largely poppycock. The Japanese have made enormous progress in trade liberalization at least during the last half dozen years. Japan's reputation on this score is poor, largely because it delayed liberalization until very late in the game. But the reputation reflects the state of affairs of four or five years ago rather than the conditions today. The situation is, after all, that Japan will shortly have only forty items under quota restrictions—and its tariffs are, by international standards, not all that high (with certain limited exceptions such as tariffs and duties on whiskey and motor cars).

The Japanese authorities miss no chance to point out the speed with which trade has been liberalized in recent years. In all fairness, it is not an unimpressive record. . . . The agricultural items still unliberalized are very much hard-core items which count in Japanese rural politics (beef, bacon, ham, some fish, milk, cream, processed cheese and oranges). The liberalization ratio (proportion of actual imports liberalized) is not a good guide to Japan's achievement; but the fact that (according to Japanese sources) Japan will have cut down to 40 restricted items by September—compare United States (only 5), Britain (25), West Germany (28) and France (70)—suggests it has not that much further to go in this area.

Businessmen who rage against Japan's failure to liberalize therefore switch their fire from quota restrictions to nontariff barriers . . . and to nonliberalization of foreign direct investment. Even on the latter, however, there are signs that the Japanese may change their fundamental thinking (no more than 50-50 ventures for foreigners) by mid-1971. It remains to be seen precisely what the Japanese will do in this area—but it could be spectacularly different, and more liberal.

THE UNITED STATES AND JAPAN ON COLLISION COURSE [9]

Back in the early 1960s, in a magnanimous gesture to one of its Asian clients, the United States agreed to hold annual cabinet-level meetings with Japan on economic matters. And the Japanese, who had just emerged from the devastation of

[9] From article in *Newsweek*. 78:37+. S. 20, '71. Copyright Newsweek, Inc. 1971. Reprinted by permission.

World War II, were appropriately grateful—even though the American delegates who came to Tokyo often dozed through the boring conferences, resting up for the round of lavish geisha parties that were thrown for them by their hosts. But when the eighth such meeting between the two nations opened . . . [in September 1971] in Washington, nobody there was caught napping. For the rapid deterioration in US-Japanese relations over the past few months turned the once-routine affair into a verbal slugging match and threatened to ignite an economic war between two of the industrial giants of the non-Communist world.

The donnybrook was, perhaps, inevitable, for in the past decade economic relations between Tokyo and Washington have come full circle. Today, the protégé has surpassed its former master in industrial efficiency and has opened an estimated annual balance-of-trade surplus of $2.8 billion in Tokyo's favor. "It's as if the United States is playing the role of the underdeveloped nation," says one economist, "supplying raw materials which the Japanese turn into manufactured products." Recognizing this fact, the Japanese cabinet officers arrived in Washington . . . confidently expecting to be treated as equals. Instead, they discovered that although they had closed the economic gap, the psychological gap between the two countries remained as wide as ever—and that the Americans still insisted on treating the Japanese like new boys in the school of global power.

This attitude on the part of the United States was strikingly illustrated by the manner in which Secretary of State William Rogers lectured the Japanese in his address to the conference. All the relevant economic indicators point to Japan's great-power status, he chided them. "But your exchange rate has remained at the parity established in 1953 when Japan was weak and vulnerable . . . while imports into your markets have been hindered by quotas and licensing requirements." Then Rogers declared: "The result in psychological terms has been resentment in business and labor circles in the United States at the restrictions on US exports and investment, and apprehension about the penetration of the US market by Japanese goods."

The Japanese . . . refused to budge. After reading an advance copy of Rogers's speech, Foreign Minister Takeo Fukuda completely rewrote his original . . . remarks. And when his turn came to speak, Fukuda gave as good as he got. He suggested that America's economic plight was due less to its trade imbalance with Japan than to the failure of its self-indulgent fiscal and monetary policies. What is more, ignoring Rogers's direct call for unilateral revaluation of the yen, the Foreign Minister warned that the United States had better revoke its recently imposed 10 percent surcharge on imports lest "other countries . . . adopt countermeasures" that might cause "the collapse of the free-trade system."

Nor was Japan's new defiance confined to economic affairs. . . . Fukuda made it abundantly clear that Japan was not likely to cosponsor two US resolutions at the United Nations . . . that are designed to admit Communist China . . . while reserving a seat for Taiwan. . . . [Premier Sato overrode his party's objections and supported the United States in its futile efforts to keep Taiwan in the UN.—Ed.]

Despite clear warnings in advance that Japan was in no mood for compromise, the United States was taken by surprise by Fukuda's stunning display of independence. Partly, this was because Japan's Prime Minister Eisaku Sato, ignoring the advice of aides, has continued to talk in public as though nothing had happened to disturb relations between Tokyo and Washington. Partly, too, Americans were simply not sufficiently aware of the new mood of assertiveness in Japan. . . .

An even more significant factor in shaping Tokyo's policies was a growing national consensus that Japan cannot afford to bail the United States out of its problems. Thus, Japanese farmers, who form the backbone of the nation's ruling Liberal Democratic Party (LDP), have warned Prime Minister Sato not to give in to US demands for quota concessions on the importation of American farm products. "If imports of these items are freed," said Agricultural Minister Munenori Akagi, "the LDP regime will collapse." And Sato's opponents within the LDP have argued—along with most Japanese business leaders—that Japan should not jeopardize its future relations with Peking by cosponsoring the US resolutions at the United Nations. Eager to up their share of the potential mainland market, these entrepreneurs contend that Tokyo would clearly be foolish to go out on a limb for Taiwan at a time when Washington was seeking closer ties with mainland China.

Aggravating this drift away from the United States on specific issues is a deep distrust of American policy that is increasingly shared by all Japanese. This feeling was engendered by Washington's recent failure to consult Tokyo on two momentous decisions that are referred to in Japan as "the Nixon shocks": the President's impending visit to Peking and his protectionist-oriented new economic plan.

The Japanese people are in great turmoil politically and psychologically [explained Edwin O. Reischauer, former American ambassador to Japan]. Their government had told them that it was consulted by the United States on all major decisions. Then along came these two devastating surprises, which damaged both the government's credibility and the nation's faith in American trustworthiness.

Despite these realities, a few optimists still claimed to find reason for hope. They pointed to Tokyo's decision . . . to make some minor concessions on its import policies. They noted that, despite the mutual recriminations that characterized the Washington meeting, both Rogers and Fukuda concluded their speeches with references to the "mutual trust" and "partnership" between the United States and Japan. And they dwelled on the banquet that followed the meeting at which Mr. Nixon and Fukuda exchanged toasts to their countries' "friendly relations."

JAPAN TRADE FACES SHARP CURTAILMENT [10]

United States trade with Japan—now $11 billion a year in exports and imports—will be sharply reduced by the emergency economic measures taken by Washington.

These include the 10 percent of additional duties that has been imposed on cars, textiles, cameras and other items that figure prominently in imports from Japan plus the extra costs of imports resulting from a devalued floating dollar.

The combined effect of these measures is calculated to cut imports from Japan by as much as $1 billion a year. And with a 10 percent upward revaluation of the yen, which the Administration hopes will be forced on Japan by the import surcharge, the reduction in imports might rise another $500 million.

These are among the main conclusions being drawn by American and Japanese traders as a result of the Nixon Administration's move to reverse the deficit that—along with other economic problems—has appeared in the United States trade balance.

Regarded as Uncertain

The Administration, however, has indicated that an upward revaluation of the yen—and of other currencies—would lead to removal of the import surcharge. But Japanese traders regard the lifting of the surcharge as uncertain and thus they believe they may have to contend with both extra duties and an upvalued yen. [The surcharge has since been lifted on textile imports.—Ed.]

But while the immediate focus is on the effects on imports from Japan, the full impact is seen as an overall contraction of trade, a reduction also in United States exports to Japan. The net effect thus may be no change in the trade balance with Japan, which . . . [in 1970] showed a deficit for this country of more than $1.2 billion.

[10] From article by Brendan Jones, staff correspondent. New York *Times.* p 40. Ag. 20, '71. © 1971 by The New York Times Company. Reprinted by permission.

In 1970, United States exports to Japan amounted to $4.6 billion—according to Commerce Department figures—and showed an increase of 33.2 percent over the 1969 volume. The main items of exports were machinery and transportation equipment (more than $1.1 billion); agricultural raw materials, grains and food (more than $1 billion); mineral fuels such as coal and coke (more than $500 million), and chemicals and other manufacturing materials (nearly $600 million).

United States imports from Japan last year amounted to $5.9 billion and were 21.2 percent higher than in 1969. Among the main items were iron and steel (nearly $900 million); electrical machinery and appliances ($980 million); cars and other motor vehicles (nearly $800 million); telecommunications equipment including TV (more than $700 million); textiles ($560 million); musical instruments ($375 million); optical goods ($160 million) and toys and food products (about $130 million each).

Decrease of 6 Percent

In the first half of 1971, United States exports to Japan totaled more than $2 billion, 6 percent less than in the first half of 1970. Imports in this period were up 32 percent to nearly $3.5 billion. A major stimulus was the threat of steel and other strikes and the actual West Coast dock strike.

For Japan, the United States accounts for 30 percent of her total exports. The United States accounts also for about 30 percent of Japan's total imports.

After Canada, Japan is the United States' largest single export market. In 1970, Japan became the first country to import more than $1 billion of American agricultural products, including large quantities of feed grains, soybeans, wheat and cotton.

Until 1965, the United States enjoyed a substantial surplus in its trade with Japan. Since then, however, there has been a growing deficit.

The rapid rise of imports from Japan in recent years, particularly in textiles, steel, cars and other consumer goods, has led to increasing demands for restrictions by domestic producers.

Together with the Nixon Administration's own efforts to restrain textile imports, demands for quotas on textiles, shoes and other products reached a climax . . . [in 1970] in legislation that just barely failed of enactment.

The new import surcharge, however, has had possibly more drastic effect on imports from Japan than would quotas. Japanese trade sources assert that the added duties alone amount to a total embargo for steel and textiles.

Major Japanese Imports From U.S.—1970

Coal-coke	$411,641,000
Oil seeds	315,013,000
Rough wood	305,811,000
Aircraft	238,414,000
Unmilled corn	235,147,000
Iron-steel (scrap)	209,186,000
Office machines	201,760,000
Unmilled wheat	157,486,000
Unmilled cereal	129,586,000
Cotton fibers	88,433,000

Major U.S. Imports From Japan—1970

Motor vehicles	$790,311,000
Telecommunications equipment	705,088,000
Iron-steel (sheets)	480,242,000
Sound recorders	375,624,000
Clothing	277,244,000
Iron-steel (tubes)	190,108,000
Textile fabrics	173,668,000
Scientific instruments	157,449,000
Office machines	145,050,000
Iron-steel (bars)	143,008,000

Source: United States Department of Commerce

IV. JAPAN AND THE WORLD

EDITOR'S INTRODUCTION

Although Japan's power, at the moment, is entirely in the economic sphere, its present and future military and political role in Asia and in relation to the rest of the world is a matter of importance. For more than twenty-five years Japan has maintained a low profile in international affairs. Now, changes are occurring and these will have significant consequences in the decade to come.

The first article in this section examines the range of issues between Japan and the United States. The most important concerns the United States—Japanese Treaty of Mutual Cooperation and Security which, it has been agreed, will extend through the 1970s. Another issue concerns the return of the Ryukyu islands to Japanese rule. A third area of controversy is in the economic sphere, with pressure for tariff protection against Japanese competition arising from American businessmen. Thus far, the United States Government has resisted such pressures, but Japan has been asked to speed up its own trade liberalization so that others may enjoy the same business advantages in Japan that the Japanese enjoy elsewhere.

The following article, from *Time* magazine, details several of the important economic issues between Tokyo and Washington. These issues revolve around textile exports from Japan, charges of dumping on the part of Japan in order to win markets, and Japan's refusal to open its own markets more freely to foreign goods.

In October 1971, the United States and Japan signed a textile pact which restricts the growth of man-made fiber and wool imports from Japan—as well as Taiwan, Hongkong, and South Korea—to an annual rate of between 5 and 7.5 percent. In return, the United States lifted its 10 percent surcharge on textiles from all countries. This surcharge had been imposed on August 15, 1971, as part of President Nixon's new economic policy to control inflation and correct the balance of payments deficit (the excess of money leaving the United States over that coming in, a condition responsible for the weakening of the dollar).

The third selection looks at the direction of Japan's Asian policies. Japan's rather considerable foreign aid efforts are examined. Its links to the Soviet Union and mainland China are reviewed, and it is pointed out that China depends heavily on Japan for certain key products. Finally, consideration is given to the possible policy options for Japan in the 1970s.

The next article also discusses Japan's role in Asia. It notes that continued Soviet occupation of the northernmost Japanese islands is a major point of contention between the two nations but that the possibility of economic collaboration nevertheless exists. As for mainland China, the article sketches the forces that draw the two nations together, as well as those that keep them apart. Lastly, this article reviews Japan's relations with the Southeast Asian countries.

The final article focuses specifically on Japanese policy as it relates to two issues: (1) the return of American occupied Japanese territory to Japan and (2) the problems and policy implications of Japanese relations with China.

JAPAN AND THE UNITED STATES [1]

There have been two [recent] developments in the Japanese-American relationship which are likely to set a pattern for events during the coming decade. In November 1969 Prime Minister Sato met with President Richard M. Nixon in Washington, D.C. In their joint communiqué they agreed to continue the United States—Japanese Treaty of Mutual

[1]From *Japan—the Risen Sun*, pamphlet by Martin E. Weinstein, assistant professor of political science, University of Illinois. (Headline Series No. 202) Foreign Policy Association. 345 E. 46th St. New York 10017. '70. p 50-60. Reprinted with permission from Headline Series #202. Copyright 1970 by the Foreign Policy Association, Inc.

Cooperation and Security into the 1970s. They also agreed that the United States would return Okinawa to Japan in 1972. The return of Okinawa represents the achievement of a long-sought Japanese foreign policy goal, and the extension of the 1960 security treaty indicates that for the foreseeable future the two governments intend to continue as military allies.

In the summer of 1970, however, the friendly, cordial atmosphere generated by the Sato-Nixon meeting was suddenly clouded by a breakdown in the negotiations . . . over the issue of "voluntary" limitations on Japanese textile exports to the United States. The Japanese were willing to agree to a one-year quota, while the Americans insisted on a five-year quota. The breakdown in the negotiations, after eighteen months of talks, coincided with moves in the United States Congress to legislate textile import quotas. [A pact, controlling the growth of Japanese textile exports to the United States, has since been signed.—Ed.]

In Japan, the collapse of the talks reflected an unexpected degree of anti-American sentiment, not among the opposition parties and press, where it is normal, but among Japanese conservative politicians and businessmen, who have been the advocates of close Japanese-American relations. The future pattern of Japanese-American relations suggested by these two events is one of political-military cooperation and economic-commercial competition. The major questions raised by these events are: first, What is the general nature of the Japanese-American relationship? and second, Will our security relationship with Japan continue to be effective or will it be undermined by commercial rivalry?

Security Relations

Since the late 1940s, both the United States and Japanese governments have believed that their national security requires an American military commitment and an American military presence in Japan and in East Asia. The Japanese government's security policy grew out of Prime Minister Yoshida's realization during 1946-47 that Japan would be militarily helpless in the United States-Soviet cold war. Mr. Yoshida and his colleagues understood that whichever of the superpowers had access to the Japanese islands and to Japanese skills and industry would enjoy a decisive military advantage in the Western Pacific and on the periphery of Northeast Asia. They concluded that Japan could best provide for its external security by allying itself with one of the superpowers. Prime Minister Yoshida and his conservative successors have rejected the Socialist policy of unarmed neutrality on the grounds that in the pinch the superpowers could not be trusted to respect that neutrality, and that, unarmed, Japan would not have the means to protect its neutrality. For Japan, then, there were two questions: Which of the superpowers should it choose as an ally? and What kind of an alliance relationship should it build?

The answer to the first question was easy for Prime Minister Yoshida to give, and easy for his successors to accept. The United States and not the Soviet Union occupied Japan after the Pacific war. Moreover, the Americans have had the naval and air power to protect the Japanese islands against Soviet attacks, while the Soviet Union, powerful as it has been on the Eurasian continent, has not had the means to protect Japan against the United States. Third, American military power not only can protect Japan itself, it can also insure Japanese access to the world's oceans, to distant sources of raw materials and fuels, and to the overseas markets necessary to Japan's viability as an industrial economy. The conservatives have also abhorred Soviet communism and preferred parliamentary, constitutional government. In short, all of Japan's prime ministers to date have believed that Japan is not able to defend itself against either of the military superpowers; that the Soviet Union cannot defend Japan against the United States; and that the United States can defend Japan against the Soviet Union.

The question of what kind of alliance relationship the Japanese have wanted to build is also understandable in simple, straightforward language. The Japanese leaders have wanted the United States to guarantee Japan's external defense and to maintain sufficient forces in the Far East to make that guarantee a credible deterrent. They have never favored an anti-Communist crusade, and they have not wanted the United States-Japanese alliance to pose an offensive threat to the Soviet Union, since in their minds such a threat would increase the possibility of a United States-Soviet war in which Japan would be a battleground. They have believed throughout the last two decades that the United States ground forces in South Korea and American naval and air superiority in the Western Pacific, together with American nuclear missiles, are a credible and effective deterrent against any hostile action in the Japan area by either the Soviet Union or Communist China. The Japanese government has wanted sufficient United States bases in Japan to maintain this disposition of forces. They have been willing to build up their own ground forces . . . and small but well-equipped air and naval forces intended to reinforce the American guarantee. Finally the Japanese government has wanted these defense arrangements to be formalized in a mutual security treaty with the United States under which the two governments would consult and act together to defend Japan.

The significance of Japan in American defense policy ought to be self-evident, but unfortunately, for many of us, it is not. Our problems in South Vietnam and with Communist China should not cause us to lose sight of the fact that Japan, because of its strategic location and industrial power, is the one nation in East Asia whose enmity or alliance with the Soviet Union or Communist China would radically alter the distribution of power in the region and sharply affect the global balance.

The American Government despite the lack of public concern, has consistently shown a keen appreciation of Japan's strategic significance. On September 8, 1951, on the day that the Treaty of Peace signed by the allied powers and Japan in San Francisco was concluded, we also entered into a security treaty with Japan. The Korean war was then in full swing, and our Government believed that Soviet aggression against Japan was a distinct possibility and could best be avoided or repelled by building a regional alliance system in Asia comparable to NATO. We wanted Japan to build a large army of 350,000 men which we could help to equip, and for Japan to join the proposed regional pact. We also wanted to maintain military bases in Japan to support operations in Korea and to help defend Japan itself.

The Japanese government, to the acute disappointment of Special Ambassador John Foster Dulles, refused to build a large army [its army numbers around 200,000—Ed.] or to join a regional security pact. Prime Minister Yoshida argued that Japan's economic weakness and new constitution precluded large-scale rearmament and made impossible Japan's participation in a regional military agreement. As a result of these differences between United States and Japanese defense policies, the 1951 security treaty amounted to little more than a base-leasing agreement. It met both governments' minimal requirements, but neither we nor the Japanese were satisfied with it. Although the United States bases in Japan provided a *de facto* guarantee of Japan's defense, the Japanese were unhappy with the treaty because it did not include an explicit guarantee and was not mutual. Our Government felt that the Japanese did not appreciate the gravity of the Soviet threat and that they were not showing enough energy in providing for their own defense.

By 1960, however, when the Treaty of Mutual Cooperation and Security was concluded, the differences which had separated the two governments were largely resolved. The armistice in Korea and Stalin's death in 1953, followed by the thawing of the cold war in the late 1950s, led Washington to believe that large-scale Japanese rearmament and a regional defense pact were not necessary for the defense of the Far East. Consequently, in the 1960 treaty the United States explicitly guaranteed Japan's defense and agreed to consult and cooperate with the Japanese government in that defense. In return, the Japanese government continued to lease bases to us in Japan, which could be used to provide logistical support to American operations throughout the Far East. In a "prior consultation" note appended to the 1960 treaty, the United States Government agreed not to use its bases in Japan for combat operations outside Japan or to introduce nuclear weapons into Japan without the prior consent of the Japanese government. Finally, it was agreed that the treaty would be binding for ten years, after which it would continue in effect unless either government gave at least one year's notice that it wished to abrogate it. As ... noted, in November 1969, President Nixon and Prime Minister Sato expressed their intention to extend the treaty indefinitely.

The United States-Japanese security relationship has suffered from public neglect in this country, but not in Japan. On the contrary, the leaders of the opposition parties and the press have devoted great amounts of time and energy to criticizing the security treaties. Although the Japanese voters have been unwilling to view the treaty as a major political issue, opinion surveys show that the security arrangements with the United States are not popular. Underlying all objections is a sense of damaged national pride. In short, there is a widespread feeling, even among conservatives, that it is unseemly for Japan to continue to depend on the United States for its defense. The Japanese government has been aware of these feelings for years. But it knows that unless it were to build its own nuclear missiles and huge conventional forces, Japan simply could not begin to defend itself against the major powers in the region. And despite their damaged national pride, most Japanese have until now been adamantly opposed to rearmament. During the past year the government signed the nuclear nonproliferation treaty, but it is not at all certain that the treaty will be ratified. The debate in Japan over ratification suggests that perhaps national pride and the desire for independence are weakening antirearmament sentiment. There is no doubt that if the Japanese decide to, they can become a major nuclear power. But doing so will mean reshaping national priorities and disturbing the relatively stable international situation in Northeast Asia. . . .

The American Government has not had to contend with public opinion, either for or against, on this matter. This has given it considerable latitude in dealing with Japan. But this lack of public interest in the United States-Japanese security relationship can turn into a disadvantage if any special-interest groups in this country should take a strong stand against our policy toward Japan.

Commercial Rivalry and Interdependence

The breakdown of the . . . negotiations on the textile quota issue suggests that there are groups in the United States—as well as in Japan—who are willing to pursue their economic interests, despite the risk to our mutual security relationship. In this country the textile manufacturers, particularly in the South, have concluded that Japanese textile imports, which have been increasing about 5 percent a year, are taking too much of the United States market. They want a voluntary self-imposed, long-term quota on Japanese exports to this country. Both the Japanese textile industry and the government have noted that Japanese textile imports amounted to less than 5 percent of the total value of sales in the United States in 1969 and that American domestic sales and wages in the textile industry have been increasing steadily since 1960 despite Japanese competition. This has led the Japanese . . . to conclude that the American Government's desire for a cutback in Japanese textile imports is motivated not so much by economic considerations as by promises President Nixon has made to southern textile manufacturers in an effort to build Republican Party support in the South. [The textile treaty signed on October 15, 1971, limits the growth of Japanese textile imports to 5 to 7.5 percent annually.—Ed.]

While the President's "southern strategy" may be a factor in our demand for a textile quota, it should be noted that during the past few years a variety of business interests in this country have been complaining about Japanese competition and restrictions. Japanese exports of steel, electronic components and hi-fi sets have had a larger impact on the American market than have textiles, and have given our electronic industry stiff competition abroad. The American automobile industry has been most concerned over the rapid growth of Japanese imports, which are six times as big as in 1966.

What has most irked our automobile, steel and computer industries is that the Japanese, while taking full advantage of American liberal trade policies to expand their markets in this country, have remained relatively restrictionist in their own trade and investment policies. [See "Japan's Remarkable Industrial Machine," in Section III, above.] It is true that Japan is much more protectionist than the United States. Since adhering to the General Agreement on Tariffs and Trade (GATT) in 1964, the Japanese have moved extremely slowly to abolish the trade quotas and investment restrictions prohibited by GATT. By their own admission they are still in violation of the agreement. Japanese officials argue that despite their economy's statistically impressive growth rate, Japanese industry is still not sufficiently well-organized and efficient to face American and European competition. The Japanese government claims that its policy is to liberalize trade and investment to keep pace with the modernization of Japanese industry.

In line with this policy, the government will announce the third round of its liberalization program this fall [1970]. The third round is expected to schedule the removal by the end of 1971 of import quotas from 60 to 124 currently restricted items. These items include machinery, textiles and farm products. Tokyo is also expected to announce the further lifting of foreign investment restrictions on 323 Japanese industries by the end of 1971, permitting foreign portfolio ownership ranging from 15 to 50 percent.

The expected pace of Japanese economic liberalization, especially in investments, does not satisfy many American businessmen, who would like to operate firms in Japan under predominantly American ownership, as they can do in England, Holland and West Germany. Most Japanese officials and businessmen, although aware of financial and technological benefits to Western Europe from American business operations, are nevertheless intent on keeping the Japanese economy under firm Japanese control.

The textile issue should be seen against this growing feeling among American businessmen that Japan has been making its phenomenal economic gains unfairly, and to some extent at American expense, and against the regrettable but understandable reluctance of the Japanese to accept the obligations conferred on them by their economic growth.

Economic Interdependence

Beyond the arguments, grievances and emotionalism that have been creeping into the United States-Japanese commercial rivalry, however, there are powerful reasons, economic as well as strategic, for keeping our overall relations cordial and cooperative. The United States is by far Japan's single largest trading partner, accounting for more than 30 percent of its total foreign trade. The Japanese know this, and it is partly because they are frustrated with their economic and strategic dependence upon us that they have been so rigid on the trade and investment issues. Japan is our second most important trading partner, after Canada, accounting for about 10 percent of total American foreign trade. Clearly, it is in both American and Japanese interests to maintain and to continue to expand our economic relations.

Officials in both governments are well aware of the importance of preserving long-term United States-Japanese security and economic ties. The danger is that emotionalism, frustration and special-interest groups in Japan as well as in the United States will generate quarrels, such as the one over textiles, that once started are extremely difficult to settle and may spill over into wider areas.

A Difficult Decade Ahead

For the Japanese, the 1970s are likely to prove more difficult than most forecasters think. Looked at from the point of view of the economists, Japan's prospects appear bright. For assuming that world trade continues to expand, the Japanese economic planners can be expected to maintain a relatively high rate of economic growth, despite the labor shortage and the infrastructure problems which beset them. It is worth keeping in mind, however, that the economist's point of view is not a comprehensive one. Conservative political leaders and bureaucrats in Tokyo can exert only a marginal influence on the world economy and on the international and domestic political conditions which they recognize are necessary prerequisites for the success of their economic policies. The political squeeze of the LDP [Liberal Democratic Party], and foreign policy and defense issues will probably require more attention during this decade, thus diverting the Japanese leaders from what until now has been their virtual preoccupation with economics. Moreover, the Japanese are learning that rapid economic growth itself generates changes in social patterns and values, which in turn affect the economy. Rapid urbanization, which is concomitant with economic growth, has contributed greatly to the erosion of the power and authority of the LDP. And as suggested by the breakdown of the textile negotiations last summer, the Japanese will have a tendency to express the self-confidence bred by prosperity in ways that could threaten to undermine the economic and security relationships with the United States that have been of central importance to Japan.

The American end of the United States-Japanese relationship suffers from public neglect. We can expect that some American business interests will continue to seek protection against Japanese economic competition and that United States Government officials, even when they oppose those business demands, will find it exceedingly difficult to resist them without public understanding of the broader issues at stake. This understanding will not develop until many more Americans realize that whatever policy we adopt in Asia in the 1970s, the feasibility of that policy will, to a large extent, depend on Japan. Above all, we will not want Japan to work against us. And unless we decide to withdraw entirely from Asia, we will need Japan's cooperation to promote peace and stability in the area.

JAPAN, INC.: WINNING THE MOST IMPORTANT BATTLE [2]

Every day, thousands of neatly dressed, briefcase-toting Japanese businessmen, technicians, engineers and salesmen swarm over the globe—inspecting, surveying, planning, advising, bargaining, buying and selling. One group is . . . in Hanoi, working on an agreement to help the North Vietnamese set up a shipping firm, textile plant and garment factory. In Zambia, geologists are surveying copper fields. On Vancouver Island, lumber men are demonstrating a new technique for cutting timber that used to be considered waste. Other groups are supervising production of Honda motorbikes in Brussels, studying sites for a hotel in Alaska and building a steel mill in South Africa, where the Japanese are considered honorary whites. In any market that arouses their interest, the Japanese use *jinkai senjitsu* (human-sea

[2] From article in *Time*. 97:44+. My. 10, '71. Reprinted by permission from *Time*, The Weekly Newsmagazine; copyright Time, Inc., 1971.

tactics), inundating the area with trade delegations and survey groups. Local businessmen sometimes feel that they are being overwhelmed by sheer force of numbers.

Fearful and resentful, European nations have built a daunting array of barriers against Japanese goods; Italy alone has forty-six import quotas directed specifically against them. Asian leaders also complain. Antonio Villegas, mayor of Manila, recently inveighed against the "insidious Nipponization of the Philippines"—then excused himself to greet a visiting delegation of Japanese advertising men. . . .

The deluge of Japanese imports is arousing an angry protectionist reaction in the United States—Tokyo's wartime conqueror turned number one trading partner. Fully 30 percent of Japan's exports go to the United States. As recently as 1964 Japan bought more than it sold in United States trade. Since then, the popularity of Sony TV's, Nikon cameras, Panasonic radios, Toyota and Datsun cars, and Honda and Yamaha motorbikes has turned the picture upside down. Materials-short Japan is a big and growing consumer of American coal, lumber and even soybeans, but in each of the past three years its sales to the United States have exceeded its purchases by more than $1 billion. The American shoe, textile, electronics and other industries have not only lost sales and profits to the Japanese but jobs as well. A member of the Nixon Cabinet voices the alarmist view held in some high Government circles: "The Japanese are still fighting the war, only now instead of a shooting war it is an economic war. Their immediate intention is to try to dominate the Pacific and then perhaps the world."

The business backlash stings Japan in many ways. The United States is negotiating tighter quotas on Japanese steel and has just agreed on a quota for stainless steel flatware. Many businessmen want the Government to go much further. Last year protectionists raced through the House a bill authorizing quotas on any foreign product that won as much as 15 percent of a United States market. The chief target: Japan. The bill died in a Senate adjournment rush, but the import debate has resurfaced this year in a way that could poison United States-Japanese political relations.

Closed-Door Policy

The most incendiary battle centers on imports of Japanese textiles. Last year they accounted for only 1.3 percent of total United States textile sales, but they have been heavily concentrated in certain segments of the market. Japanese sweaters and woolen fabrics increasingly infiltrate the United States market, and imports of man-made fibers from the Far East soared 75 percent in the first two months of . . . [1971]; probably a third came from Japan.

President Nixon in 1968 promised protection to the politically powerful southern textile industry. Two months ago, the Japan Textile Federation offered to limit shipments to the United States for three years starting July 1; they would rise only 5 percent the first year and 6 percent in each of the next two years. Those limits were not stiff enough to satisfy US trade hawks, and Nixon turned the offer down. [The new textile treaty, therefore, may not satisfy US textile manufacturers.—Ed.] The President then further tangled the textile situation by mixing it up with international politics. He decided to submit to the Senate a treaty returning Okinawa to Japan, rather than handing it back by administrative action as he had led Tokyo to expect. If the southern textile bloc can sew up thirty-four Senate votes, it can defeat the treaty. Okinawa is such an emotional issue in Japan that a defeat could topple Prime Minister Sato's government.

As the political snag over textiles shows, the dangers of a United States-Japanese trade split go far beyond economics. Japan has been the greatest force for postwar stability and progress in Asia, largely because its industrialists have channeled the vigor of the Japanese people into peaceful pursuit of markets. If that Japanese trait is denied commercial expression, it could explode in frustration. Averting a United States—Japanese blowup will require a much deeper understanding of the nature of the friction than either side has shown so far. Many Japanese leaders play down the American resentment as being largely a consequence of the 1970 US recession, and they figure that it will fade as business continues to revive....

In fact, the US reaction reflects more than pain in the pocketbook. American executives are enraged by what they regard as Japan's refusal to observe the rules of the game of world trade. Many American businessmen contend, with some justification, that the Japanese dump not only TV sets but also steel, textiles, float glass and radio tuners. US industrialists also complain bitterly (and enviously) about the special help their Japanese rivals get from the Tokyo government: official blessings for cartels formed to win big foreign orders, lavish and extensive government-financed studies of which overseas markets might be easiest to crack, low-interest loans to exporters from the government-dominated banking system, and the lowest corporate taxes in the industrial world.

Most of all, Americans are incensed by the way that Japan, while invading foreign markets, has closed its domestic economy to many foreign goods and most foreign capital investment. Supposedly, that situation is changing. In 1969, Tokyo maintained quotas or other barriers against 120 categories of imports. Last January [1971], the number was cut to 80, and this month [May] it is supposed to go to 60; the Japanese have pledged to reduce it to 40 by September. They also promise to open nearly all their "pureblood" industries to either 50 percent or 100 percent foreign ownership by August 1.

Clogs, Not Cars

Even after the next stage of liberalization, foreigners will not be able to send in many products—including unlimited quantities of oranges and some airplanes and machinery— or to invest in the manufacturing of large computers, certain electronic items and petrochemicals. The Japanese government rejects many investment applications, stalls on others, attaches unacceptable conditions to still others. Ford and Chrysler have been delayed for years in attempts to buy into the booming Japanese auto industry, and General Motors has won permission for only a limited investment: 35 percent ownership of a joint venture with Isuzu Motors, a truck maker. Says James Adachi, president of the American Chamber of Commerce in Japan: "We can set up a factory to make *geta* [Japanese wooden clogs], or open a supermarket, so long as it is smaller than 500 square meters."

Inscrutable Economics

The real cause of the present strain is that the United States is confronting something totally new in the world: a mighty industrial economy that has been shaped by Oriental history and psychology. If Japan does not follow the gentlemanly trade rules, it is not because of simple greed but because it does not adhere to Western principles on much of anything. To outsiders the Japanese economy seems inscrutable in ways alternately amusing and shocking.

Industry is cartelized to a point that would make John D. Rockefeller envious. Companies carry a burden of bank debts that would drive a US executive to drink—or his company to the brink. Above all, every part of the Japanese economy is directed toward a national goal, and almost everybody feels a sense of participation in achieving it. Bureaucrats, bankers, business executives, workers—all labor hard to make Japan a world power through economics.

As a first step, Japan must quickly take down the bamboo screen that blocks high-technology imports and foreign investment. Many Japanese industrialists tirelessly contend that their economy is an "adolescent" that needs protection against the big, rich, "mature" competitors of North America and Europe, but that argument clearly is not valid today, Japanese manufacturers also have an unnatural price advantage in world competition because their currency, the yen, is undervalued. Tokyo economists reluctantly concede that the yen must be revalued upward; there is likely to be a 5 percent revaluation within a year.

On the United States side, the prime requisite is to develop a coherent trade policy aimed at expanding the flow of world commerce and investment and protecting only those domestic industries that are necessary for the nation's economic or military security. As a painful corollary, the United States may have to permit some nonessential industries to be overwhelmed by foreign competition. Washington at present has no overall policy, but tries to tackle trade problems one by one as they pop up. A sensible step would be to accept the Japan Textile Federation's unilateral offer to restrict cloth shipments to the United States. It is absurd for the United States and Japan to squabble fiercely over textiles, because that industry is not vital to the economy of either nation. Simultaneously, the United States could crack down harder on dumping in several industries, perhaps by flatly embargoing shipments, though it would be much wiser to do that on a company-by-company basis rather than by blanket rulings as in the TV case.

President Nixon's ability to develop a comprehensive policy is severely limited because he lacks legislative authority to negotiate new US trade concessions in return for a lowering of foreign barriers. That authority expired in 1967; the Administration should demand that Congress renew it. Armed with such power, Nixon could call for a new world trade conference similar to the successful Kennedy Round of 1964-67, this time aimed at elimination of nontariff barriers to trade and investment. This conference would be an ideal forum in which to press the Japanese to remove their remaining restrictions. In return the United States should try to persuade European nations to wipe out their restrictions on Japanese goods.

The West's Turn to Copy

A mutual lowering of barriers will temporarily make Japanese competition more intense but also more equitable.

Sooner or later Japan will have to temper its export drive because its economy is already operating under some severe strains. For one thing, the country is running out of labor. A decade ago, there were two job openings for each high school graduate; this spring there are 7.7. Japan has also bought export growth largely at the price of skimping on internal investment in housing, roads and pollution control. The country's industrial pollution is perhaps the world's worst. Says Nippon Steel's Nagano: "We need more roads, harbors, bridges, housing. People are living two families to a six-mat (9 ft. by 12 ft.) room. In advanced Western countries, industrial production and the production of social capital have been balanced, but we have been so busy exporting that we have not balanced these things."

Instead of fighting the Japanese, US businessmen can join with them in some mutual projects to make money and, incidentally, help out the have-nots of the world. Harold Scott, director of the United States Bureau of International Commerce, believes that as Japan's labor shortage worsens, its industrialists will gradually shift their stress from exports to American-style overseas investment. US companies could speed the process by proposing joint ventures with Japanese firms in third-country markets. Scott envisions, for example, a combination of US and Japanese timber companies to develop the huge lumber resources of the Upper Amazon.

US businessmen could also learn a few lessons from the Japanese system. Its labor practices, for example, are both humane and efficient. Some of them might be tried in the United States—not lifetime one-company employment, of course, but perhaps some training practices. Japanese industrialists train many of their workers in several skills rather than insisting on greater specialization as their Western counterparts do. A Japanese engineer is encouraged and even expected to learn something about accounting, finance and personnel work. This seems to help produce better-rounded, more mobile and more highly motivated workers than are found in many Western factories and offices.

A society as heterogeneous and individualistic as the United States probably cannot rally most of its people behind a national economic goal in the Japanese sense. But Japan has shown that business and government do not have to consider each other as adversaries, as they often do in the United States. Though the United States certainly should not cartelize its industry Japanese-style, Japan's success might stimulate some thinking in Washington as to whether the antitrust laws should be liberalized to promote the nation's competitiveness in world markets.

Needed: More Japans

In any program of trade cooperation with Japan, the United States can count on support from some of the biggest Japanese businessmen. Morita [of Sony] has been calling for Japan to open its industry more rapidly to US investment, though he gives the idea a characteristic Japanese twist of self-interest: "If we allow more US investment, we will not need a security treaty. . . . Of course the Americans will protect us then. Everybody protects his property."

Morita also proposes international harmonization of product standards, safety regulations, antipollution laws and food standards in order to equalize costs and guard against the possibility that differing national rules will be used to keep out foreign goods. Beyond that, he has begun to believe that the world's industrial leaders have been too narrow in their trade thinking. "There are three big industrial areas: the United States, Japan and Europe," he says. "Now we have manufacturers trying to sell each other the same things. It doesn't make sense. Two thirds of the world's people are still living under low standards, and because of that they do not yet constitute a viable market. Just as the United States helped Japan rise from nothing, we should all join to try to make more Japans in other parts of the world." That is a sound if ambitious program, and an example of the kind of thinking that may well solve United States—Japanese trade difficulties. The issue—and the real Japanese challenge—is nothing less than whether the two mightiest trading nations in the world can learn to live in commercial peace.

NEW ASIAN ROLE FOR THE RISING SUN? [3]

At the moment it is hard to discern the direction of Japan's Asian policies. The Japanese, tiring of their "low posture" in global affairs and prodded by their friends (especially the United States) to carry greater regional responsibilities, are debating how to attain a more influential stature among their neighbors.

Foreign Aid or Export Promotion?

Not even Japan's severest critics would accuse it of neglecting its needy neighbors. It is now the world's fourth biggest donor of foreign aid, if official and unofficial sources are combined. Of the ... [about $650 million given annually in recent years] about 48 percent was given through government channels and the rest in the form of private loans, investment and export credits. And the bulk of Japanese aid goes to Asia.

Yet one hears criticisms. The money is given grudgingly; a Southeast Asian grumbles that aid "is offered to us by the United States but we have to request it from Tokyo." Tokyo is now contributing slightly under the 1 percent of national income suggested to rich donor nations by the UN (although the US contribution is even less). There has been little technical assistance. Most loans are on "hard" terms (high interest rates, short repayment periods). Loans and credits are concentrated in such countries as Taiwan and South Korea, which afford lucrative markets for Japanese goods.

All in all, concludes one wry observer, "Japan doesn't have a foreign aid program, it only has an export-promotion program." ...

[3] From "A Great Power Role for the Rich Man of Asia?" *Great Decisions 1970*. Foreign Policy Association. 345 E. 46th St. New York 10017. p 58-60. Reprinted with permission from *Great Decisions 1970*. Topic #5. Copyright 1970 by the Foreign Policy Association, Inc.

Criticisms of the "ungenerous" Japanese could . . . be rebutted by pointing to their regional-development efforts of several years' standing. They have matched the US contribution of $200 million to the Asian Development Bank. They are participating in the UN-sponsored project to develop the Mekong river basin. They themselves initiated the nine-nation Southeast Asian ministerial conference. Tokyo has sponsored courses for Asians in small-industry management, has supplied free training in Japan to over nine thousand students from developing countries and has sent some five hundred of its own "peace corps" volunteers to work in those countries.

Channels to the Communists

In their relations with the rest of Asia, the Japanese emphatically do not wish to be identified as militant anti-Communists. They regard coexistence and cooperation with their Communist neighbors, above all with the two giants facing them on the mainland, as being in Japan's best interests.

Japan and the Soviet Union have yet to sign a formal treaty ending their three weeks of hostilities in August 1945 (although the state of war was declared terminated in 1956) because Japan disputes the continuing Soviet occupation of the Kurile island chain and southern Sakhalin island. Both territories were promised to Stalin at the Yalta conference in return for his country's belated entry into the Pacific war.

Japan's claims—particularly to the Kuriles, which most jurists agree have been legally Japanese since 1875—may also have proved a stumbling block to less-formal collaboration: plans for joint Soviet-Japanese industrial development of Siberia have barely got off the ground. Nevertheless, the two countries sustain a brisk commerce. The USSR became Japan's fifth largest trading partner in 1968 and is expected to supply a growing share of its coal and oil imports.

Tokyo's trade pipeline to Peking, on the other hand, has narrowed conspicuously since China's economy was disrupted by Mao's Cultural Revolution. (Until 1967 trade, tourism and other exchanges flourished despite the diplomatic vacuum; Tokyo officially recognizes only the Nationalist Chinese regime in Taiwan.) Even so, Japan remains Communist China's main commercial channel to the outside world. Each capital accords diplomatic courtesies to the other's "private" trade mission, and the actual trade volume . . . [about $570 million in 1970—Ed.] always exceeds the annual written agreement.

The Chinese, while denouncing Japan's "subservience to American imperialism," depend heavily on its shipments of steel and machinery. And the Japanese, while deriving small gain from their current business with China, dream of a vast and fruitful exchange when the mainland giant eventually settles down to the serious pursuit of modernization. The Sato government can count on broad popular support for this "forward-looking posture" and its efforts to keep the slender pipeline open.

Model for Modernization?

Does Japan perhaps have something more to offer its Asian neighbors than trade, aid and technical assistance? Can they hope to emulate its example of successful modernization without a loss of their Asian identity and national culture?

This is the fond hope of a number of analysts. They see a grand design for Asian progress in which Japan would simultaneously serve as (1) a prototype for the smaller Asian states, (2) a less direct but constructive influence on the large, complex societies of India, Pakistan, Indonesia and even mainland China, and (3) a bridge between developing Asia and the other developed Pacific nations—the United States, Canada, Australia, New Zealand—with which Japan's own links will continue to multiply.

But other analysts see flaws in this design which could retard, if not rule out, a pivotal Japanese role in regional development.

They ascribe Japan's success as an industrial society (in which a dwindling minority of the labor force works in agriculture) to a rare combination of nature and national history. The model has little relevance, they feel, for Asian societies which are overwhelmingly agrarian, often ethnically divided and politically unstable.

Moreover, the Japanese are seen as identifying themselves primarily with the advanced (i.e. non-Asian) peoples. They cannot conceal a contempt for the other, more "backward" Asians, even though they may feel a vague racial and cultural kinship with them. . . .

Nor is the language barrier a trivial one. The Japanese are not gifted linguists, perhaps because learning to read and write their own language is so extraordinarily difficult. (A high school graduate must have memorized 1,800 characters, a college student needs twice as many.) They get by among foreigners as best they can with English.

But a much more stubborn obstacle to Japanese leadership in regional development is the remembrance of their last such attempt: the Greater East Asia Coprosperity Sphere. This was Tokyo's euphemism for the ruthless conquest and exploitation of its neighbors in World War II. Understandably, the bitter memory lingers on. So does Asian wariness of any blazing new initiatives under the flag of the Rising Sun.

How High a Posture?

The Japanese respect these fears and see various other reasons, foreign and domestic, for approaching a more ambitious foreign policy with caution. From their current debate, and the appraisals of well-informed observers, emerge three broad alternatives for the 1970s:

Introspective inactivity. Quite possibly the Japanese will forgo more ambitious policies abroad—economic leadership, political or military initiatives—in favor of what they call "my-home-ism": improving and enjoying life in Japan. "The Japanese, despite a few tentative and cautious moves toward regional cooperation, are absorbed more than ever in their own domestic problems," writes . . . [an] American correspondent and former diplomat. Over the next decade, he believes, their extra revenues will be spent not on foreign aid or defense but on roads and schools, hospitals and housing: "This is not a nation that is about to embark on a drive to influence the rest of Asia."

In strategic terms, this self-absorbed passivity would be compatible with either (1) a continued alliance with the United States, letting the latter continue to bear the main burden for Japan's conventional defense, or (2) a Nehru-like nonalignment policy—which need not exclude the ultimate safeguard of the American nuclear deterrent.

A major pole of Asian-Pacific power. In the opinion of Robert E. Osgood of Johns Hopkins University, "it would certainly be one of the great anomalies of history if a state with the potential power, the extensive foreign interests, the long-run security problem, and the national vitality of Japan should indefinitely entrust the military protection of its interests to another state. . . ." A school of Japanese political analysts sometimes called the "new realists" agrees. Japan's natural and proper role is that of an active participant in great-power politics. This means building a credible military force—certainly with conventional weapons, perhaps with nuclear arms as well.

Furthermore, the Japanese must consider the possible danger of nuclear blackmail by Communist China. They are concerned with the strategic protection of the Strait of Malacca, a vital waterway for their Middle Eastern oil imports, once the British military forces are withdrawn from Singapore in the early 1970s. The possibility of Soviet adventurism in the Far East also cannot be excluded.

This high military-political posture could lean in one of two directions: (1) A more equally balanced military partnership between Japan and the United States. The American alliance would act as a constraint on Japan's resurgent power and help allay Asian qualms about a revival of aggressive Japanese militarism; (2) an independently nationalistic Japan, pursuing alignments and policies which would not necessarily coincide with America's. In a rough analogy to the Atlantic alliance, Japan might develop the equivalent of a Gaullist "third force," as opposed to playing the role of a Western European "twin pillar" in a balanced NATO partnership with the United States.

Nonmilitary international influence. A third course for Japan would lie between the first two: an expanding role in the economic and political affairs of the Asian-Pacific region *without* commensurate military influence.

The . . . [Self-Defense Forces] could continue improving in quality, with perhaps a modest increase in quantity and function (such as serving with a UN peacekeeping force). "However," believes . . . a former United States Foreign Service officer, "Japan will not assume security responsibilities outside of the country nor enter pacts of a military nature. A military role in Asia for Japan is out of the question for a long time to come, and, indeed, if it were to develop, would destroy many of Japan's constructive economic accomplishments in Southeast Asia."

Further constructive accomplishments might be promoted through a "Pacific Community" of aid donors—a consortium of the advanced Pacific nations—and through Asian regional groupings in which Japan, Australia and New Zealand would be influential members. At the same time, a diplomatically independent Japan, subservient to neither of the two superpowers, could help lessen the gulf between China and the outside world.

This might, of course, lead to a more neutralist Japanese foreign policy than at present. Or, Tokyo might maintain a free-world orientation as an admittedly very junior partner in US strategic planning. In either event, Japan would offer no military threat to its neighbors—and suffer no military drain on its profits.

JAPAN AND ASIA [4]

The most pronounced change in Japan's national life since World War II has probably been in its foreign relations. In the years just before World War II, it was an article of faith among the Japanese that their country's military security and economic well-being necessitated a colonial empire in Asia which included Taiwan, Korea and the southern half of Sakhalin; a satellite state in Manchuria; and special commercial and military privileges in China. There were some bold men in those days who suggested that Japan could maintain its vital economic interests in Asia by peaceful rather than military means. But even these men firmly believed that Japan's security and prosperity rested on the preservation of its "special and unique interests" on the Asian continent. Indeed, between 1920 and 1940, about one quarter of Japan's foreign trade was with China.

Following its defeat and surrender in 1945, Japan lost all of its territorial possessions in the Far East, as well as its commercial position in China. And yet . . . Japan has enjoyed unprecedented prosperity and a high degree of political stability and military security. The Japanese experience in Asia suggests that what appear to be natural and permanent overseas interests can turn out to be quite ephemeral and dispensable.

Nevertheless, during the last twenty years, the opposition parties, many journalists and a minority of conservatives have been calling for the "normalization" of Japan's relations with its Asian neighbors. In theory, the government has also favored normalization. In practice, however, it has moved very slowly and cautiously, fully aware of the constraints placed upon it by the cold war, as well as the unhappy legacy in Asia of Japan's pre—World War II colonial and military policies.

[4] From *Japan—The Risen Sun*, pamphlet by Martin E. Weinstein, assistant professor of political science, University of Illinois. (Headline Series No. 202) Foreign Policy Association. 345 E. 46th St. 10017. '70. p 43-9. Reprinted with permission from Headline Series #202. Copyright 1970 by the Foreign Policy Association, Inc.

Relations With the Soviet Union

Japanese policy toward the Soviet Union has been shaped primarily by considerations of national security and only to a limited extent by economics. Since the end of World War II, the government has viewed the Soviet Union as the principal military threat to Japan. This does not mean that Japan's leaders have believed that a Soviet attack is an imminent, overwhelming danger. But it does mean that the government has looked upon the United States–Japanese security treaties as deterrents to Soviet aggression, and that Japan's limited forces have been concentrated on Hokkaido, to protect against a Soviet thrust from the north. Moreover, the government's policy has been consistent with public attitudes. Over the past two decades, opinion polls have consistently shown that among the Japanese public the Soviet Union is the most disliked of all foreign states.

The animosity between the Japanese and the Russians can be traced back to the late nineteenth century, when they began a struggle for control in Korea and Manchuria, a struggle in which Japan held the upper hand until the end of World War II. Then, in the summer of 1945, disregarding the Japanese-Soviet Neutrality Treaty of 1940, the Russians took advantage of Japan's military collapse. Soviet troops drove the Japanese out of Manchuria and northern Korea, and occupied southern Sakhalin and the entire Kurile island chain, including the northern islands of Etorofu, Kunashiri, Habomai and Shikotan, off the coast of Hokkaido, over which they had no claim, historical or otherwise. Finally, Stalin demanded but did not get a Soviet zone of occupation in northern Hokkaido.

From the Japanese point of view, the Soviet occupation of the northern islands continues to be an illegal and unjustified intrusion on Japanese territory. The Soviet Union did not adhere to the 1951 San Francisco peace treaty, and until 1956, Japan and the Soviet Union were legally at war. In 1956, after almost two years of difficult negotiations, all that the Japanese and Soviet governments could agree on was to formally end the state of war and to reestablish diplomatic relations. The Soviet Union still maintains garrisons on the northern islands, and the Japanese government still insists that a peace settlement with the Soviet Union must include the return of the islands to Japan.

Despite this territorial dispute, however, and despite the pronounced anti-Communist cast of Japan's ruling conservatives, the two governments have found limited areas of agreement. The Japanese fishing industry considers the waters north of Hokkaido to be indispensable and has been instrumental in getting the government to negotiate yearly fishery agreements with the Soviet Union.

Japan's trade with the Soviet Union has never amounted to more than 2 percent of its total foreign trade. For over a decade now, since the Sino-Soviet rift became pronounced, the Soviet Union has been suggesting that Japanese capital and technology would be welcome in the development of Eastern Siberia, and has hinted that Japan could have access to the oil and natural gas resources of the region. Negotiations on Siberian developments have been held intermittently, but to date they have not borne much fruit.

Sino-Japanese Relations

Japan's relations with Communist China are not markedly closer or more friendly than its relations with the Soviet Union, but their tone and flavor are quite different. In 1951, following the conclusion of the San Francisco peace settlement, Japan signed a peace treaty with the Nationalist government on Taiwan. The Japanese continue to recognize and to trade with the Nationalists, and as a result they have no formal diplomatic relations with the Communist government in Peking.

For many Japanese, including some prominent conservatives, their estrangement from China is a source of deep regret. Despite the tremendous differences in their present styles of living, and social and political systems, there is a feeling in Japan of racial and cultural affinity with China, which is mixed with a sense of guilt over Japanese aggression in China in the 1930s and 1940s. Chinese nuclear tests and the excesses of the Cultural Revolution have dampened Japanese sympathies, but there is little animosity or fear of China among the Japanese.

Trade with mainland China has followed an erratic pattern. On occasion it has grown slightly larger than trade with the Soviet Union, only to drop off virtually to zero when Peking, for reasons that are not entirely clear, has decided to stop it. At the present time, trade is again on the upswing, following the decline that accompanied the Cultural Revolution. The Japanese government, as well as businessmen and economic planners, hope that political conditions in China will stabilize, and that in the future Peking will want to broaden political and commercial contacts with Japan. For the time being, however, they feel that they can get along quite well without China's friendship or trade, and they are reluctant to make any political concessions to Peking for the sake of expanded trade.

Japanese-Korean Relations

In Japanese-Korean relations, the legacy of Japanese colonialism has been a more powerful factor than the cold war. From 1910 until 1945, Korea was under Japanese rule. The Japanese built railroads and factories and improved Korean agriculture, but they looked down on the Koreans as an inferior people—lazy, corrupt and badly organized. The Koreans grew to resent and hate their arrogant Japanese rulers and developed a strong nationalist movement, which the Japanese repeatedly and cruelly suppressed.

The mutual distrust and ill-feeling bred by the colonial experience was so great that despite the Korean war and despite strong American pressure for Japanese-Korean cooperation, Japan and the Republic of Korea did not even establish diplomatic relations until 1965. The Japanese have had limited contact and trade with North Korea, but no diplomatic relations. In recent years, Japanese trade and investments in South Korea have grown rapidly and have been an important factor in South Korea's economic growth.

The Japanese government's chief concern in Korea has been that the peninsula not be under the control of a hostile, Communist power—either the Soviet Union or Communist China. It has, of course, been out of the question for Japan itself to intervene politically or militarily in Korea. The government has considered, however, that the American defense commitment to South Korea protects Japan's security interests, and it has always looked upon American military facilities in Japan as logistical support bases for combat operations in Korea—although this is not understood by most Japanese.

Japan and Southeast Asia

The most positive and promising of Japan's foreign relations in Asia are in the region stretching south from Taiwan, around the Indochina peninsula, through Indonesia and toward Oceania. Although the states in the region are often lumped together under a Southeast Asia label, they are highly diverse in terms of economic development and in political cohesion and stability. In the aftermath of World War II, however, all the Southeast Asian peoples had in common a fear of Japanese military conquest born of their wartime experience. Japanese policy in the region has been aimed at dissipating this fear and suspicion and at the expansion of Japan's trade and investments.

The first steps toward both of these goals were taken in the 1950s, when Japan reached reparation agreements with Burma, the Philippines, Indonesia and the Republic of Vietnam. Under these agreements, the states that had suffered war damages received compensation, much of it in the form of machinery and long-term credit, which also stimulated Japan's export industries. In the late 1950s and early 1960s, Japan's economic planners encouraged the creation by commercial firms of markets and raw material sources in Southeast Asia through credit arrangements and a variety of loans and investments. Japanese efforts during this second phase were intended primarily to meet the needs of Japanese industry and gave little consideration to requirements of the local economies.

Since 1965, however, the Japanese government has shown a growing awareness that Japan's economic interests will be best served by programs that also enhance the economic development of the Southeast Asian states. In keeping with this more enlightened view of their self-interest, the Japanese government was an active participant in establishing the Asian Development Bank and took the initiative in forming the Southeast Asia Ministerial Economic Development Conference. Through these instruments, the Japanese government is trying to direct development funds where they will do the most good for the recipient states as well as for Japanese businessmen. Japan's foreign aid in Asia—including loans and investment—has increased from $248 million in 1964 to $650 million in 1969. Well over half of Japan's total foreign aid goes to Southeast Asia. [See also "Japan and the Region" in Section III, above.—Ed.]

While the absolute volume and value of Japan's trade with Southeast Asia has grown steadily and rapidly over the past fifteen years, it is worth noting that Southeast Asia's share of Japan's total exports has dropped from over 40 percent in 1955, to less than 30 percent today. This relative decline of Japan's trade in Southeast Asia reflects the extraordinary rise in Japanese exports to the more developed states, especially the United States, Canada and Australia.

A most interesting aspect of Japan's economic relations with Southeast Asia is related to the labor shortage in Japan. . . . This shortage, and the rapid increase in wages in Japan, has probably done at least as much to stimulate industrial growth in Southeast Asia as have Japanese investments and loans. During the past five years, industries in Taiwan, Thailand and Singapore, where labor is plentiful and cheap,

have become competitive with Japan in the manufacture of
footwear, rubber products, batteries and even transistor
radios. Because of the labor shortage, it is now cheaper for
the Japanese to import these items than to make them at
home. Moreover, the growing shortage of Japanese labor
and the availability of cheap and increasingly skilled labor
in Southeast Asia are likely to attract a growing volume of
Japanese investments away from Japanese industry into
Southeast Asia.

For the future, a major question is whether Japan's growing economic involvement in Southeast Asia is again going
to create political tensions, either between the Japanese and
Southeast Asians, or between the Japanese and the other
peoples who have economic and political interests in this
region.

TIME FOR A MACHIAVELLI TOUCH [5]

Okinawa and China will be the major foreign policy issues facing Japan this year [1971] and next. Each issue has
a material bearing on the other in that they are inseparably
linked with the Asia policy of the United States. Indeed, the
United States will continue to be the common denominator
in all Japanese foreign policy operations. While it would
be wrong to assume Japan blindly follows Washington's
dictates, it would be equally wrong to presume that Japan
can act independently of American policy.

Clashes between Tokyo and Washington, particularly in
trade and economic fields, symbolize Japanese efforts to gain
equal status in its relations with the United States and the
equally strong American efforts to preserve the status quo
characterized by the euphemism "complete policy identity."
But the United States still holds the whip hand in ties with
Japan.

It is in this context that the reversion of Okinawa to
Japan will have to be viewed. The question is not if Okinawa

[5] From article by Koji Nakamura, journalist. *Far Eastern Economic Review*. 71:45-8. Mr. 27, '71. Reprinted by permission.

can be returned by the promised time of 1972 but how it can be returned. While there was a "perfect identity of views" between President Richard Nixon and Prime Minister Eisaku Sato—their joint communiqué issued late in 1969 said the reversion would mean complete integration of Okinawa into the United States—Japan Security Treaty arrangements—subsequent developments have raised doubts about the disposition of the huge defense structure the United States maintains in Okinawa.

The most controversial issue is whether Okinawa can remain free of nuclear weapons. Foreign Office circles have admitted no such agreement will be incorporated in the reversion documents to be sanctioned by the legislative branches of the two countries. They have pointed out that since nuclear questions in the United States fall within the President's mandate, a conflict would arise if such a question had to be cleared by the Senate, not to speak of the Japanese Diet.

While Prime Minister Eisaku Sato and Defense Agency chief Yasuhiro Nakasone have declared publicly that Japan may inspect the bases after the reversion to confirm nuclear weapons have been removed from the islands, it is highly doubtful if the United States would ever agree to such a policing arrangement. Another factor, to date not raised, is if seaborne nuclear facilities operating in Okinawan waters would conflict with the "denuclearization" arrangement. It is widely known that nuclear-equipped Poseidon submarines will soon operate in Asian waters if, indeed, they do not do so already.

A more basic consideration is whether or not, as far as American Asia strategy is concerned, Okinawa has lost the strategic value it had in the past. It is strongly argued that Okinawa's reversion to Japan is to be effected not so much because of Japanese demands but because of the island's lessening importance in American defense plans in Asia. The land-based nuclear facilities could well be replaced by seaborne equipment.

If Okinawa has lost the strategic value, complete, nuclear-free reversion can be expected, but if the "administrative" reversion is an expedient stemming from the mounting demand for the United States to get out, both the American and Japanese governments will be creating problems rather than reducing them.

Such doubts and suspicions will have to be clarified in the course of reversion negotiations . . . in progress in Tokyo. The draft reversion documents, which will probably assume the character of a treaty, will be . . . referred to the US and Japanese legislatures in September [1971] or later. Yet, little attention has been paid to the provision stipulated in the joint communiqué that reversion could be "renegotiated" if the Vietnam war were still in progress at the time of the scheduled reversion.

While government sources have dismissed any possibility of a change in the reversion timetable, unpredictable developments in Indochina could affect the situation, particularly in relation to China's position should the war widen.

Since Japan's China policy is a reflection of Sino-American relations, Okinawa's future is particularly relevant as the base's structure is directed against China even though at the moment it caters more to the Vietnam war. While Okinawa to China could be what Cuba was to the United States during the nuclear crisis some ten years ago, there is no indication at the moment that China would force removal of American military potential in Okinawa, nuclear or otherwise. But there is reason to believe Okinawa's use can materially affect China's policy not only towards Japan but the United States.

Military matters alone, however, will not determine the flavor of Japanese policy toward China. It will be essentially a political decision by Tokyo on Taiwan.

Recent trade and political talks between Japanese delegations and Chinese officials—including Premier Chou En-lai—clearly indicated that Taiwan alone was deterring normalization of Sino-Japanese relations and, by inference, the

United States—Japan Security Treaty did not have to be abrogated as a condition of such arrangement. While it is inconceivable that the Japanese government under Sato would abrogate the Taiwan-Japan Peace Treaty, an appreciable and perceptible change has emerged in the thinking of Japan's political leadership on the China issue.

A policy change is most unlikely, as long as Sato remains in office; the Foreign Ministry will most likely adhere to the "important question" formula which would stipulate that expulsion of Taiwan would also need a two-thirds majority of the UN General Assembly. [In October 1971 Japan co-sponsored the defeated US resolution to keep Taiwan in the UN.—Ed.]

Strongly anti-Peking economic and political forces, including American and South Korean interests, have renewed campaigns in defense of Taiwan where Japan has an estimated investment of more than $600 million—annual trade between the two countries also totals $600 million.

But growing pro-Peking, or not-anti-Peking, sentiment is symbolized by the formation of a supra-partisan parliamentary group favoring normalization of relations with China. Led by ex-Foreign Minister Aiichiro Fujiyama who has just returned from Peking as head of a private political mission, the group represents a majority of membership of the two houses.

Prime Minister Sato himself is not unconcerned with China. He even has had a private adviser to brief him on recent developments revolving around China. He was quoted as telling intimate associates that the "biggest factor in the China issue is Generalissimo Chiang Kai-shek."

Those charging Japanese behavior in China is "humiliatingly low postured" have lost ground since the alleged low posture is now thought to be, in essence, economic tactics rather than the reflection of a political principle. While elements of humility may be necessary in view of the Japanese presence in China in the thirties and forties, Japanese feel China will need Japanese economic assistance more than Japan needs China's potential.

But there is equal recognition that Japan will have to face formidable competition from other industrial nations, eventually including the United States, and the comfortable trade position ($820 million in commodity exchanges in 1970 when Japan was China's biggest trade partner) it enjoys today may be challenged anytime should the China market be exposed to freer international competition.

While the China issue will thus polarize national opinion more sharply rather than unify it, Japan increasingly realizes it has committed a grave error in foreign policy on China and the United States—it has failed in the past to use one country as a counterbalance against the other.

While nothing tangible has emerged, Foreign Ministry officials are known to be seriously weighing the advisability of exploiting relations with the Soviet Union. It is possible that as long as Washington remains basically nonhostile to Moscow, Russia's shadow over Sino-Japanese relations might conceivably strengthen Japan's hand in dealing with Peking.

It will be a supreme challenge to the capability of a foreign office which, for long, has been an administrative agency, rather than a political tactician with the Machiavellian expertise that guides contemporary power politics.

BIBLIOGRAPHY

An asterisk (*) preceding a reference indicates that the article or a part of it has been reprinted in this book.

BOOKS, PAMPHLETS, AND DOCUMENTS

Allen, G. C. Japan's economic expansion. Oxford. '65.

Beasley, W. G. The modern history of Japan. Praeger. '63.

Benedict, Ruth. The chrysanthemum and the sword. Houghton. '46.

Brannen, N. S. Sōka gakki: Japan's militant Buddhists. John Knox Press. '68.

Brooks, Lester. Behind Japan's surrender. McGraw-Hill. '68.

Buck, P. S. The people of Japan. Hale. '68.

Burks, A. W. The government of Japan. Crowell. '61.

Dore, R. P. ed. Aspects of social change in modern Japan. Princeton University Press. '67.

*Foreign Policy Association. Great decisions 1970. The Association. 345 E. 46th St. New York 10017. '70.

   Reprinted in this book: Excerpts from Fact Sheet No. 5. A great power role for the rich man of Asia? p51-62.

Glazer, Herbert. The international businessman in Japan. Tuttle. '68.

Guillain, Robert. The Japanese challenge. Lippincott. '70.

Hall, J. W. and Beardsley, R. K. Twelve doors to Japan. McGraw-Hill. '65.

Halloran, Richard. Japan: images and realities. Knopf. '69.

Hellmann, D. C. Japanese foreign policy and domestic politics. University of California Press. '69.

Hersey, John. Hiroshima. Knopf. '46.

Huh, Kyung-mo. Japan's trade in Asia. Praeger. '66.

Hunsberger, W. S. Japan and the United States in world trade. Harper. '64.

Hürlimann, Martin and King, F. H. Japan. Thames (London). '70.

*Japan. Ministry of Foreign Affairs. Public Information Bureau. Facts about Japan. The Bureau. Tokyo. '69.

*Japan. Ministry of Foreign Affairs. Public Information Bureau. New tasks for Japan. The Bureau. Tokyo. '69.

Kahn, Herman. The emerging Japanese superstate. Prentice-Hall. '70.

Kawai, Kazuo. Japan's American interlude. University of Chicago Press. '60.

Kurihara, K. K. The growth potential of the Japanese economy. Johns Hopkins Press. '71.

Lockwood, W. W. The economic development of Japan. Princeton University Press. '68.

Maddison, Angus. Economic growth in Japan and the U.S.S.R. G. Allen. '69.

Maruyama, Masao. Thought and behaviour in modern Japanese politics. Oxford. '63.

Okamoto, Shumpei. The Japanese oligarchy and the Russo-Japanese war. Columbia University Press. '70.

Olson, L. A. Japan in postwar Asia. Praeger. '70.

Passin, Herbert, ed. The United States and Japan. Prentice-Hall. '66.

Reischauer, E. O. Japan past and present. Knopf. '64.

Reischauer, E. O. Japan; the story of a nation. Knopf. '70.

Reischauer, E. O. The United States and Japan. Harvard University Press. '65.

Seidensticker, E. G. and the editors of Life. Japan. (Life World Lib.) Time. '61.

Stone, P. B. Japan surges ahead: the story of an economic miracle. Praeger. '69.

Thayer, N. B. How the conservatives rule Japan. Princeton University Press. '69.

Toland, John. The rising sun; the decline of the Japanese empire, 1936-1945. Random House. '70.

Webb, Herschel. An introduction to Japan. Columbia University Press. '55.

*Weinstein, M. E. Japan—the risen sun. (Headline Series No. 202) Foreign Policy Association. 345 E. 46th St. New York 10017. '70.

Weinstein, M. E. Japan's postwar defense policy: 1947-1968. Columbia University Press. '71.

PERIODICALS

Annals of the American Academy of Political and Social Science. 370:133-42. Mr. '67. Japanese character in the twentieth century. D. G. Harind.

Architectural Record. 148:109-28. S. '70. New developments in Japanese architecture; with introduction by M. F. Schmertz.

Asian Survey. 9:703-21. S. '69. Strains in current Japanese-American defense cooperation. Frank Langdon.

Asian Survey. 9:900-18. D. '69. Japan's trade with Communist China. G. P. Jan.

Asian Survey. 10:765-78. S. '70. Japan and the nuclear non-proliferation treaty. G. H. Quester.

Atlantic. 225:14+. Ap. '70. Reports: Japan. M. H. Halperin.

Atlantic. 227:78-82+. Mr. '71. Japan, the land of the re-rising sun. Ross Terrill.

Atlas. 19:32-3. F. '70. Must power come from the barrel of a gun. Peter Grubbe.

Atlas. 19:21. Je. '70. What's behind Japan's high school radicals. Kiyoaki Murata.

Aviation Week. 92:56. Mr. 9, '70. Japan's aerospace future grows brighter.

Bulletin of the Atomic Scientists. 25:2-7. My. '69. Non-proliferation treaty and Japan. Ryukichi Imai.

Bulletin of the Atomic Scientists. 26:35-9. Je. '70. Japan and the nuclear age. Ryukichi Imai.

Bulletin of the Atomic Scientists. 26:107-15. Je. '70. Scientists and the decision to bomb Japan. D. H. Frisch.

Bulletin of the Atomic Scientists. 26:32-4. S. '70. Memory and a hope: Hiroshima after a quarter century. D. W. Schriver, Jr.

Business Week. p 116+. F. 27, '65. Japan puts out small welcome mat.

Business Week. p 75-7+. Ag. 21, '65. As Osaka goes, so goes Japan.

Business Week. p 76-8. Ja. 8, '66. Japan's giant web of world traders; trading companies serve as export-import agents for manufacturers.

Business Week. p 82-4+. O. 1, '66. Yamaka's potpourri finds a market; motorcycles, skis, pianos hit it big in U.S.

Business Week. p 108+. My. 24, '69. Japan's trade giant picks old U.S. hand. Sueyuki Wakasugi.

Business Week. p 124-6. S. 6, '69. Sharp side of the rising sun.

Business Week. p 67-8. D. 6, '69. Japanese head for a bout with inflation.

*Business Week. p 59-65+. Mr. 7, '70. Japan's remarkable industrial machine.

Business Week. p 88-9+. My. 16, '70. Japan: now the imitator shows the way.

Business Week. p 54. My. 23, '70. Tokyo makes Wall Street toe the line.

Business Week. p 43. Je. 6, '70. Mitsubishi made in the U.S.

Business Week. p 72-4. Ag. 1, '70. Here comes Hitachi, hot for foreign sales.

Business Week. p 44. Ag. 22, '70. Wage boom busts Japan's small business.

Business Week. p 22-3. S. 5, '70. Enter the quiet Japanese, on the run.

Business Week. p 44-6. O. 10, '70. Japanese banks flex their muscles.

Business Week. p 32-3. D. 26, '70. Japanese set sail for New York.

Business Week. p 82-3. Ja. 9, '71. Trade squabble puts Sato on the spot.

Business Week. p 26. Mr. 20, '71. Japanese textile curbs may get a trial.

Business Week. p 68. Mr. 20, '71. Japanese face suit for dumping TV sets.

Catholic World. 207:53-6. My. '68. Japan: blueprint for the future: interview; ed. by C. K. Palms. W. A. Givotaers.

Christian Century. 82:1612+. D. 29, '65. Japan-Korea accords. G. K. Chapman.

Christian Century. 83:333-4. Mr. 16, '66. New left in Japan. P. G. Altback.

Commonweal. 94:34-6. Mr. 19, '71. Politics of suicide; Mishima's seppuku. R. T. Halloran.

Contemporary Review. 215:140-2. S. '69. Rural voter in Japan. R. L. Brown.

Contemporary Review. 216:175-7. Ap. '70. Japan's 21st century: some possible trends. R. L. Brown.

Current History. 49:284-93. N. '65. Japan's role in south Asia. Theodore McNelly.

Current History. 58:202-8+. Ap. '70. U.S.-Japanese treaty crisis. Robert Epp.

Department of State Bulletin. 53:770-7. N. 15, '65. U.S.-Japanese trends and prospects; address, October 30, 1965. W. P. Bundy.

Department of State Bulletin. 53:777-80. N. 15, '65. Japan and the United States: the essentials of partnership; address, October 25, 1965. W. P. Bundy.

Department of State Bulletin. 60:447-50. My. 26, '69. Japan's economic dynamism and our common interests in East Asia; excerpts from address, March 18, '69. R. W. Barnett.

Department of State Bulletin. 61:401-3. N. 10, '69. United States—Japanese relations today; address, October 22, 1969. U. A. Johnson.

Economist. 233:38+. N. 29, '69. Army grows up.

Economist. 233:21-2. D. 27, '69. Japan: growth as before.

Economist. 234:66-8. Mr. 14, '70. Guiding the risen sun.

Economist. 235:39-40. Ap. 4, '70. Armed forces raise their head.

*Far Eastern Economic Review. 71:25-72. Mr. 27, '71. Japan 1971.
   Reprinted in this book: Looking beyond the boom. John Roberts.
   p 41-4; Time for a Machiavelli touch. K. Nakamura. p 45-8; Economic
   invasion myth. H. S. Stokes. p 49-50; Japan and the region. Christopher
   Beck and others. p 51-70.

Forbes. 104:36. N. 15, '69. View from the Pole; Alaska's best
   customer.

Forbes. 106:28-31+. N. 1, '70. Pacific basin.

Forbes. 106:35. N. 1, '70. Looking ahead in Asia; interview. Saburo
   Okita.

Foreign Affairs. 44:90-9. O. '65. Political movements in Japan.
   Nobusuke Kishi.

Foreign Affairs. 44:253-63. Ja. '66. Japan in neutral. P. W. Quigg.

Foreign Affairs. 45:215-28. Ja. '67. Our dialogue with Japan. E. O.
   Reischauer.

Foreign Affairs. 46:193-204. O. '67. Living with the real Japan.
   G. R. Packard.

Foreign Affairs. 47:509-20. Ap. '69. Japan beyond 1970. Kei
   Wakaizumi.

Foreign Affairs. 48:21-38. O. '69. Japan's legacy and destiny of
   change. Kiichi Aichi.

Foreign Affairs. 48:344-57. Ja. '70. Japanese culture and the business boom. H. F. Van Zandt.

Fortune. 71:54+. Mr. '65. Hands across the China Sea.

Fortune. 74:66+. S. '66. Warriors of Hitachi. J. L. Schecter.

Fortune. 76:126-9+. N. '67. Why Japan's growth is different. Max
   Ways.

Fortune. 80:33-4. Jl. '69. Japan opens its doors, just a bit.

Fortune. 80:100-2+. Ag. 1, '69. What manner of men are these
   Japanese? Carl Mydans and Shelley Mydans.

Fortune. 82:126-31+. S. '70. How the Japanese mount that export
   blitz. Louis Kraar.

Fortune. 83:98-9+. F. '71. Japan will have to slow down. Nobutane
   Kiuchi.

Geographical Review. 60:264-7. Ap. '70. Keeping up with Japan.
   J. D. Eyre.

Harper's Bazaar. 101:72+. Mr. '68. Japan's inland sea. James
   Egan.

Harper's Bazaar. 103:60+. F. '70. All's fair in Japan. Marion
   Gough.

Harper's Bazaar. 103:194-5+. Mr. '70. Invitation to Japan. Bernard
   Rudofsky.

Harvard Business Review. 48:45-56. N. '70. How to negotiate in
   Japan. H. F. Van Zandt.

Holiday. 47:46-9. F. '70. Kyoto, Osaka's exotic neighbour. J. R.
   Roberson.

Life. 63:4. D. 8, '67. Role for Japan to live up to.

Life. 68:44-6. Mr. 27, '70. How the Japanese got so much so fast. J. K. Jessup.

Life. 69:30-1. Jl. 31, '70. Twenty-five years ago: two cities, two bombs.

Look. 29:17-20. Ag. 10, '65. Japan. Frank Gibney.

Look. 31:28-33. F. 7, '67. Henri Cartier-Bresson's Japan.

Look. 33:27-42+. O. 21, '69. Japan '70; symposium.

Look. 33:28-9. D. 21, '69. New face of world power. Frank Gibney.

Look. 34:38-45. Ag. 11, '70. Hiroshima. Norman Cousins.

Nation. 202:479-80. Ap. 25, '66. Japan: co-prosperity again. Albert Alexbank.

Nation. 206:82-4. Ja. 15, '68. Japan in Asia's future. W. M. Ball.

Nation. 209:374-9. O. 13, '69. Japan 1970: year of upheaval. J. P. Freed.

Nation. 211:293-5. O. 5, '70. Passing the buck to Tokyo.

National Geographic Magazine. 131:268-96. F. '67. Japan's sky people, the vanishing Ainu. M. I. Hilger.

National Geographic Magazine. 132:295-337. S. '67. Kayak odyssey from the inland sea to Tokyo. Dan Dimancescu.

National Geographic Magazine. 137:295-339. Mr. '70. Kansai: Japan's historic heartland. T. J. Abercrombie.

National Review. 22:1118-20. O. 20, '70. Rising sun. David Brudnoy.

National Review. 22:1349-50. D. 15, '70. How stable is Japan? Gerhart Niemeyer.

Natural History. 75:16-25. O. '66. Vanishing Ainu of north Japan. Shin'inchiro Takakura.

New Republic. 154:12-13. Ja. 15, '66. Japan: the reluctant ally against China.

New Republic. 154:19-22. Mr. 5, '66. Japan plays the field; peace and trade with everyone. Alex Campbell.

New Republic. 160:11-13. Je. 14, '69. Why we're returning Okinawa to Japan. Alex Campbell.

New Republic. 161:16-18. Jl. 5, '69. Sun up in Asia. Alex Campbell.

New York Times. p 1+. F. 28, '71. For Japan, the future is now. A. M. Rosenthal.

*New York Times. p 1+. Mr. 26, '71. New breed of big trust in Japan. Takashi Oka.

New York Times. p 1+. Jl. 6, '71. Sato reorganizes cabinet and asks better U.S. ties. Takashi Oka.

New York Times. p 55. Jl. 28, '71. GATT economic study sees Japan ending bogeyman role. Victor Lusinchi.

New York Times. p 1+. Ag. 10, '71. Chou looks to broad talks with Nixon. James Reston.

New York Times. p 6. Ag. 11, '71. Sato aide seeks rapport with U.S. Takashi Oka.

New York Times. p 28. Ag. 13, '71. Trade war with Japan? [editorial]

New York Times. p 3. Ag. 16, '71. China's charges of militarism worry Japan.

New York Times. p E 32. Ag. 20, '71. Squeeze on Japan.

*New York Times. p 40. Ag. 20, '71. Japan trade faces sharp curtailment. Brendan Jones.

New York Times. p 22. Ag. 25, '71. Tokyo says yen can be revalued only as part of a global currency realignment. Takashi Oka.

New York Times. p 15. S. 23, '71. Sato under fire for China stand. Richard Halloran.

New York Times. p 13. O. 20, '71. Bigger voice in U.N. sought by Japanese. Emerson Chapin.

New York Times. p E 2. O. 11, '71. "Nixon shocks" may jolt Sato right out of office. Richard Halloran.

New York Times. p 1+. N. 11, '71. Senate endorses Okinawa treaty; votes 84 to 6 for island's return to Japan. J. W. Finney.

New York Times Magazine. p 26-7+. Mr. 6, '66. All is one, one is none, none is all. Phillip Kapleau.

New York Times Magazine. p 34-5+. O. 16, '66. Japan is one of the biggest countries in the world. E. O. Reischauer.

New York Times Magazine. p 30-1+. Ap. 6, '69. Okinawa, mon amour. Takashi Oka.

New York Times Magazine. p 48-9+. N. 16, '69. Premier Sato would trip his way across a stone bridge to make sure it was safe. Takashi Oka.

New York Times Magazine. p 22-3+. F. 22, '70. Going to the fair? how to understand the Japanese. D. L. Osborn.

New York Times Magazine. p 5-7+. Ag. 30, '70. Twenty-five years ago: how Japan won the war. Faubion Bowers.
    Discussion. New York Times Magazine. p 136-7. S. 13, '70.

New York Times Magazine. p 12-13+. F. 28, '71. Japan's self-defense force wins a skirmish with the past. Takashi Oka.

Newsweek. 65:74-5. F. 15, '65. Super shipbuilders.

Newsweek. 65:80-2. My. 17, '65. How to succeed in business in Japan.

Newsweek. 68:67-9. Ag. 15, '66. Back-door war; profiting from Vietnam war.

Newsweek. 70:36-8. O. 2, '67. Grand tour, Japanese style: emergence of a superpower.

Newsweek. 72:52+. N. 25, '68. Japan in search of Japan.

Newsweek. 74:30-1. Ag. 11, '69. Invitation to greatness; U.S. pressure assumes some responsibility for the security and welfare of the Pacific region.

Newsweek. 74:68+. N. 17, '69. Thinking the unthinkable.

Newsweek. 75:25-6. Ja. 5, '70. Awaiting the explosion. Bernard Krisher.

*Newsweek. 75:64-8. Mr. 9, '70. Japan—salesman to the world.

Newsweek. 75:80+. Mr. 23, '70. Growing battle of trade barriers.

Newsweek. 75:99. Mr. 30, '70. Foul ball in Japan; investigation into prizes, bribes and gambling.

Newsweek. 75:40+. Ap. 13, '70. Fly me to Pyongyang.

Newsweek. 75:75. Ap. 13, '70. Russians are coming? promoting Russian products in Japan.

Newsweek. 75:58+. Ap. 20, '70. New devil figure.

Newsweek. 76:41-2. Jl. 6, '70. Era of friction? demonstration against the U.S.-Japan security treaty.

Newsweek. 76:71. Ag. 17, '70. Free trade. Milton Friedman.

Newsweek. 76:73. O. 5, '70. Dumping: an old ban imposed anew.

Newsweek. 76:80-1. N. 9, '70. Fraying miracle.

Newsweek. 77:63-4. F. 15, '71. Japanese boom.

Newsweek. 77:79. Mr. 22, '71. Nixon's rebuff to Japan.

Newsweek. 77:84+. Mr. 29, '71. Turn of the screw.

*Newsweek. 78:37+. S. 20, '71. The U.S. and Japan on collision course.

Reader's Digest. 91:116-20. Ag. '67. Japan's quiet war against Mao. Lester Velie.

Reader's Digest. 96:77-81. F. '70. Hidden crisis in Asia. E. O. Reischauer.

Reader's Digest. 97:103-7. Ag. '70. Japan, all Asia watches and wonders. C. T. Rowan.

Reporter. 33:28-30. S. 23, '65. Political price of Japan's China trade. J. L. Schecter.

Reporter. 34:35-7. Ja. 13, '66. Japan's non-military buildup. Albert Axelbank.

Reporter. 36:31-3. My. 18, '67. Japan's new bid for leadership. J. L. Schecter.

Saturday Review. 51:20+. Ja. 13, '68. Japanese notebook. Henry Brandon.

Saturday Review. 51:40-2. Ja. 20, '68. Getting boiled in Japan; bathing. Margaret Bennett.

Saturday Review. 52:46-7. Mr. 15, '69. Hamaya's Japan. M. R. Weiss.

Saturday Review. 52:70+. S. 13, '69. Yes, the Orient hasn't changed. Michael Berry.

Science. 167:264-7. Ja. 16, '70. Japan III: industrial research struggles to close the gap. P. M. Boffey.

Science. 167:960-2. F. 13, '70. Japan: a crowded nation wants to boost its birthrate. P. M. Boffey.

Science News. 96:152. Ag. 23, '69. Linking the East; Pan-American bus and train routes. Stuart Griffin.

Science News. 97:396. Ap. 18, '70. Grappling with crowding. Stuart Griffin.

Science News. 97:516. My. 23, '70. Japan asks for help. Stuart Griffin.

Scientific America. 222:31-7. Mr. '70. Economic growth of Japan. J. C. Abegglen.

Sunset. 140:102-7. My. '68. Japanese garden designer at work.

Time. 86:78-9. Jl. 2, '65. Salesman san on safari, challenging area: Africa.

Time. 86:40+. D. 10, '65. Growing defense force.

Time. 93:82. My. 30, '69. Hard bargaining with Japan.

Time. 94:71-2. Jl. 4, '69. Showdown in trade with Japan.

Time. 94:69B-70. Ag. 1, '69. Japan's struggle to cope with plenty.

Time. 94:37. N. 28, '69. Agreement on Okinawa.

Time. 95:51-2. Ja. 5, '70. West Germany v. Japan.

Time. 95:20+. Mr. 2, '70. Toward the Japanese century.

Time. 95:26. Mr. 2, '70. New invasion of Greater East Asia.

Time. 96:40. D. 28, '70. Buddha v. pollution.

Time. 97:69-71. Mr. 15, '71. Screens against the wind, byōbu. Robert Hughes.

Time. 97:80+. Mr. 15, '71. Scramble for supplies.

Time. 97:14+. Mr. 29, '71. Of mills, textiles and Okinawa.

Time. 97:54+. Mr. 29, '71. Learning by doing.

*Time. 97:84-9. My. 10, '71. Japan, Inc.: winning the most important battle.

Time. 98:26-8+. N. 8, '71. China: a stinging victory [in the UN].

Trans-Action. 6:32-6. Ja. '69. Japanese howdunit. Martin Bronfenbrenner.

Travel. 124:52-7. O. '65. Travel's picture portfolio.

Travel. 128:45-8. N. '67. Japan's unknown side: from Shimonoseki to Aomoi. Stuart Griffin.

Travel & Camera. 32:87-90+. F. '69. Japan in transition; one hundred years of modernization.

Travel & Camera. 32:48-85+. O. '69. Japan on view; symposium.

Travel & Camera. 36:66-7+. O. '69. Japan's most closely watched train. Richard Joseph.

U.S. Camera. 28:42-5+. Je. '65. Japan. R. S. Eisley.

U.S. Camera. 28:56-9+. Je. '65. How good is Japanese equipment?

U.S. News & World Report. 58:113-14. My. 24, '65. As Japan's miracle begins to fade.

U.S. News & World Report. 60:50-3. Mr. 28, '66. Japan: the hope in Asia?

U.S. News & World Report. 61:58-62. Ag. 8, '66. Miracle of Japan: where is it headed now? interview; ed. by K. M. Chrysler. E. O. Reischauer.

U.S. News & World Report. 62:58-60. Ja. 16, '67. Two island nations: a study in contrasts.

U.S. News & World Report. 63:90-1. Jl. 24, '67. Japan's new idea for co-prosperity sphere.

U.S. News & World Report. 64:64-5. Mr. 25, '68. Japan's changing role in Asia.

U.S. News & World Report. 66:92-3. Je. 2, '69. Conglomerate way of life in Japan.

U.S. News & World Report. 67:62-3. Jl. 7, '69. Japan's U.S.-style boom, and U.S.-style problems.

U.S. News & World Report. 67:84-5. N. 24, '69. U.S., Japan on a collision course?

U.S. News & World Report. 68:26-8. Ap. 6, '70. Japan's drive to outstrip U.S.

*U.S. News & World Report. 68:42-3. Je. 1, '70. Japan: now no. 2 in autos, trucks and going for no. 1.

U.S. News & World Report. 69:66-9. Ag. 3, '70. Asia on the move: a first-hand report. C. S. Faltz, Jr.

U.S. News & World Report. 69:54-6. Ag. 10, '70. A-bombed cities: twenty-five years later. K. M. Chrysler.

U.S. News & World Report. 69:72. N. 9, '70. U.S.-Japanese trade: Sato on a tightrope.

U.S. News & World Report. 70:55. Ja. 4, '71. U.S. steps up troop cuts in Far East.

U.S. News & World Report. 70:60-3. Ap. 26, '71. Japan's drive to pass U.S. as top industrial power.

*Unesco Courier. 21:4-73. S. '68. Japan: a century of change; symposium.
    Reprinted in this book: Emperor Meiji—father of modern Japan. Ki Kimura. p 4+; From chrysanthemum to electronic computer. p 24-7; Tokyo—a tale of two cities. W. A. Robson. p 49-50+.

Vital Speeches of the Day. 37:390-2. Ap. 15, '71. Pacific trade challenge; address, March 15, 1971. Nobuhiko Ushiba.

Western Political Quarterly. 22:605-21. S. '69. Japanese people and Japan's policy toward Communist China. G. P. Jan.

World Today. 26:325-33. Ag. '70. Options for Japan in the 1970s. Richard Storry.